FLEE TO THE MOUNTAINS

THE CHURCH'S RESPONSIBILITY TO ISRAEL IN THE FINAL 7 YEARS OF THE AGE

CHRISTOPHER MANTEI

CONTRIBUTIONS BY:

*JOEL RICHARDSON, JAKE MCCANDLESS,
FRED LONDON, ISRAEL POCHTAR*

FLEE TO THE MOUNTAINS

Copyright © 2019 by Christopher Mantei

Wings Of The Eagle, LLC

All rights reserved. No part of this book may be reproduced or transmitted in any form or by any means without written permission from the author.

Cover: Jo Ann Eshleman

Maps: Mark Davidson

Printed in USA

Wings Of The Eagle

מקלט יעקב

Jacob's Refuge

EndTime.
Church

Flee To The Mountains is not a novel.
It's not a work of fiction.
It's not a theory.
It's real.

ACKNOWLEDGEMENTS

First to Ashley. My wife, my best friend and help-meet. Many rewards are surely coming her way for sticking by my side, I know it has not been anything approaching easy. I am daily thankful to our God for her and the life He has allowed for us. Looking forward to that Day when we can rest and enjoy this earth together. Our sons are so blessed and loved.

Jake McCandless for his assistance and encouragement in writing this book, and for his Brotherhood and pastoral leadership to myself and many others. It seems like we have known each other for decades now, though it has only been since 2017!

Joel Richardson for his ministry of countless helps - known and unknown - in this book and many other endeavors. His simultaneous heart for the Church, the Jews and Muslims is continuously inspirational to me.

Mark Davidson for the maps you see in chapter 5. Also for his friendship and being used by the Lord to write the seminal "Daniel Revisited" and other works for the Church.

Mary Beth, a tireless warrior locally and globally. She is an intense lover of Israel and the Jewish people. I'm pretty sure she has been to Israel more times than I have hairs left on my head! Her selfless dedication to Jesus is the greatest I've seen in person; the Spirit of God in her was obvious from the first time I was in the room with her. Very much looking forward to what God will have her do next.

Randy Scott, my Pastor and fervent supporter. The blessings of having such a "to the point" example of love with no fear and of service with no complaint are too great to put on paper. So very thankful the Lord has brought him into my life!

Fred London and Israel Pochtar. Their generosity in providing rich, compelling dialogue truly made this book complete.

Last but not least, my Mom. Her simple wisdom of my childhood, "Give God your best and He will bless you" has been a lifelong companion. She is just a personification of unconditional love and support.

CONTENTS

Preface

PART 1: MAKING THE CASE

1. It will happen - and far from hopeless
   "Let the reader understand"
2. Establishing the Facts
   "I will provoke you to jealousy by those who are not a nation"
3. Israel Fleeing to the Mountains throughout the Bible
   "Surely the Lord God does nothing, unless He reveals His secret to His servants the prophets"

PART 2: REALIZATIONS

4. Realization: the What
   "The people who know their God shall be strong, and carry out great exploits. And those of the people who understand shall instruct many"
5. Realization: the Where
   "These shall escape from his hand: Edom, Moab, and the prominent people of Ammon"
6. Realization: the Why - Back to Sinai
   "I did not go up to Jerusalem...instead I went to Arabia"

PART 3: WHAT WE MUST UN-DO

7. Misunderstanding: God will do this without the Church
   "Great fear came upon all the church and upon all who heard these things"

8. Misapplication: Fleeing to the West
   "For whom the LORD loves He corrects, Just as a father the son in whom he delights"
9. Mistrust: refusing to work together as one Body
   "We should not trust in ourselves but in God who raises the dead"

PART 4: WHAT WE MUST DO

10. Hear what the Spirit is saying to the Church
    "The Holy Spirit says: today, if you will hear His voice, do not harden your hearts as in the rebellion, in the day of trial in the wilderness"

End Notes/Links

*A note on quotations from the Bible in this book. Several versions were used throughout, including the NKJV, NASB, NIV, CSB and ESV. There are so many quotations and references I felt it better to just list them here and not in the chapters themselves. I realize this is an unorthodox method of Bible version citation, but as you will see, this book is different. I figure anything that drives us into the Word of God is a good thing.

Holy Bible: The New King James Version. 1982. Nashville: Thomas Nelson.
Holy Bible: New American Standard Bible. 1995. LaHabra, CA: The Lockman Foundation.
The Holy Bible: New international version, containing the Old Testament and the New Testament. (1978). Grand Rapids: Zondervan Bible Publishers.
Holy Bible: Holman Christian Standard Version. 2009. Nashville: Holman Bible Publishers.
ESV Study Bible. English Standard Version, Crossway, 2011.

PREFACE

Let's get this conversation going

A note to any pastors, clergy and other ministry leaders reading this work: first, thank you! I know your time is precious. Second, this book is an invitation to get a conversation started. I submit to you that the "Time of Jacob's Trouble" is an incredibly pertinent and crucial matter, but almost no one in the Church of Jesus Christ is talking about it. Our calling as shepherds, stewards, servants, entrusted with the very Word of God in the Spirit of God compels us to thoughtfully consider this great question. And then once we consider it and hear the confirming voice of Holy Scripture, to act on it. In teamwork, unity, humility, and courage…to whatever end He permits.

What you are about to read is the fruit of nearly 30 years of Christian study, research, learning, teaching, network building, interviews, forerunning ministry and pastoring of congregations. I had resisted for years to write these things in book form as, frankly, my discipline in writing is atrocious. But, as the calendar turned to 2019, a new urgency took hold and with the encouragement of my friend and fellow traveler Pastor Jake McCandless, the work of "putting it all down on paper" commenced. So, I now ask for your kind indulgence (and preemptively for your forgiveness) as these chapters that follow are not necessarily easy to digest and may run afoul of your present understanding of certain Biblical topics and events. It is in the spirit of conversational camaraderie that I humbly submit these words to you.

All Glory to the One True God - the God of Israel - Father, Son, Holy Spirit. In the service of Jesus the Messiah and of His body, the Church. Without Him I could do nothing.

Your Brother,

Christopher Mantei

Associate Pastor, Iron Faith Fellowship
Co-Pastor, Endtime.Church
President, Wings Of The Eagle

#Maranatha

PART 1: MAKING THE CASE

Chapter 1

IT WILL HAPPEN
– AND FAR FROM HOPELESS

"Let the reader understand"

One day not so long ago, a man 1,000 miles from home was studying the Bible and praying to his God: the God of Israel. After years of confusion, this man finally understood the words given to a Biblical prophet regarding his long lost homeland, and he cried out to God for forgiveness for the sins of his nation. He now realized the disaster that had befallen his home was a direct fulfillment of warnings God had given centuries before. This man knew his God was a God of mercy and love, but now, the man saw God's severity in righteous judgment. His tear-soaked prayer ended with the acknowledgement that the nation and land and city he was praying for was not his, but God's. In this moment of brokenness, the reality of he and his people's direct dependence on their God hit home. Without God, they could not achieve victory over their enemies. Without Him to intervene and save them, they had no hope. Without Him, they could do nothing. Once their utter need for God's salvation was acknowledged, powerful revelation came. It came in more vivid detail than anyone could ever imagine.

Daniel the prophet is this repentant prayerful man. It is my belief that he was given prophetic revelation at least in part because of his simple humility and willingness to take on corporate responsibility for the sins of his own people, crying out in repentance for all of them. Daniel prayed for his people, the Jews. He prayed for his land, Judea, and for his city, Jerusalem. He prayed for a certain temple in the center of that city; a temple that stood on a high hill, meant to house his God, but instead was invaded and desecrated by an enemy. We read of this prayer and the highly specific revelation that followed in Daniel, chapter nine.

The angel Gabriel—yes the same Gabriel who told Mary that she would conceive Jesus— was sent to Daniel with perhaps the most detailed account of future events ever given to mankind. This account is so detailed that later generations mocked the very idea that they had been told everything that was to take place before the events happened. What Daniel was told was not only the precise order of events to come, but the specific amount of time it would be until the Savior of Israel—this same Jesus— would come and all those things Daniel was praying for would come to pass: the restoration of the Kingdom to Israel, the establishment of Jerusalem as the glorious capital of restored creation and the King Messiah enthroned in its rebuilt Temple. Gabriel told Daniel there would be 490 years from the command to rebuild Jerusalem until all these things would be done. But the Messiah would come and be put to death after only 483 of those years. Two details are given that probably utterly shocked Daniel: the first being that the Messiah must die, and the second, the matter of the time lapse between this event and the remaining seven years.

THE STORY ISN'T OVER

Whether we are ready to acknowledge this or not, the world has now arrived at that same intersection of decision, fact and faith. The events of the crucifixion and resurrection of the Messiah ended the 483rd year of Daniel's prophecy. We await the events foretold for the final seven, and the conditions specifically laid out by Daniel for their fulfillment appear to have aligned.

For most of the past 2,000 years (the "Church age" as it were), Bible students have, frankly, floundered to mine for alternative interpretations or understandings of those seven years, because, shortly after Jesus departed for heaven, the entirety of the Temple, the city of Jerusalem and nation-state of Israel itself, were destroyed in 70AD. Daniel makes it clear that certain events will take place in the Temple, so the destruction of the Temple challenged scholars, as they wondered if perhaps the destruction pointed towards those final years either meaning something "non-literal" or perhaps even that these events have already been fulfilled. But then, in the 20th century, God intervened to set us straight.

The horrors of Hitler in World War II cemented a decades-long push for the re-establishment of a Jewish state back in the land of Israel, and in 1948 the nation of Israel was literally restored to the map in the same place it abandoned 2,000 years earlier. Then, in 1967, the city of Jerusalem returned to Jewish hands (albeit in a tenuous "shared" capacity). All that remains is the construction of a new Temple for the events of the final seven years to be possible.

Try to put yourself in the shoes of a Jew of Daniel's day over 500 years before Jesus was born. They were exiled to a foreign kingdom, their home nation virtually wiped out, their once glorious capital city was in ruins, and their temple empty. Even as it began to be rebuilt under Ezra and Nehemiah, it must have all seemed like such a long way off. To top it all off, when the Persians who allowed this reconstruction to take place were replaced by the empire of Alexander the Great and they themselves were subsequently replaced by Rome, the voices of the prophets ceased. Once again, it seemed that God had departed, that He no longer cared for the plight of His people. But a chosen few kept the flame of the Word alive and wouldn't you know it, right on time, a man named Yeshua (Jesus) came to save Israel and all who would believe by willingly dying on a cross. It is because of that promised time of bringing in "whosoever will" from the Gentile nations that there is a "gap" between the end of the 483 years and the beginning of the final seven. That gap exists that the Gospel might go forth. And rest assured, when "the fullness of the Gentiles" has come in, the 70th Week of Daniel—that final seven years—will take place.

For the past few decades, Christians from around the world have experienced a renaissance of interest in Bible prophecy, specifically on the lynchpin text of Daniel 9:26-27. This is without question a direct work of the Holy Spirit of the God of Israel. The implication—if you haven't realized it yet—is that we in 2019 are in the MIDDLE of the story. We are not looking back at a completed drama. On a personal note, this is the word the Lord gave to me at eight years old: the story is not over, there is still more to come, and we as the Church have a part yet to play. This is what Gabriel told that praying man Daniel is still to come for us:

> *The people of the ruler who will come will destroy the city and the sanctuary. The end will come like a flood: war will continue until the end, and desolations have been decreed. He will confirm a covenant with many for one 'seven.' In the middle of the 'seven' he will put an end to sacrifice and offering. And at the temple he will set up an abomination that causes desolation, until the end that is decreed is poured out on him (Daniel 9:26-27).*

DO WE BELIEVE JESUS?

All the words of Jesus are true. As Christians we should accept this fact readily. That means all of the "red letters," including everything He spoke about the days before His return. His words are correct down to the smallest detail. Therefore, His plain message in Matthew 24:16, Mark 13:14 and Luke 21:21 must cut us to the heart and shake us awake:

> *When you see Jerusalem surrounded by armies, then know that its desolation is near; when you see the abomination of desolation, spoken of by Daniel the prophet, standing in the holy place (let*

> <u>*the reader understand*</u>*), then let those who are in Judea flee to the mountains, let those who are in the midst of her depart, and let not those who are in the country enter her. For these are the days of vengeance, that all things which are written may be fulfilled.*

Since all the evidence we have shows that the Gospels were not written down until just before 70AD at the earliest (and were not copied/distributed until years afterward), Jesus simply could not have been referring to events of the first century. What good would it do to issue a warning that nobody could read until after they happened? This would mean our God is a liar. As we know this is not the case, the only logical explanation is that the Lord Jesus Himself brought you and I into the Bible; that we are among "the readers" who are told to "understand!" And not only did He bring in a far off future generation, but simultaneously transported an Old Testament prophet who died 500 years before into today's world. He made Daniel part of the New Testament; a critical piece—perhaps the critical piece—for discerning the signs of the times.

So if all of the words of Jesus are true, why haven't we as the Church given this "breaking news of tomorrow" far more careful thought and taken action to prepare for it? Yes, fellow Christian, it will happen. There will come a day when the actual city of Jerusalem will be surrounded by the armies of the Antichrist. The day is coming when the nation of Israel will be invaded by the very nations they will make an agreement with. And yes, Israel once again will be broken, physically and spiritually. God will allow all of this to fulfill His perfect will and Word. As we will see in chapter three, the Bible is full of references to this coming period of time and what He expects His people to be doing.

Students of Bible prophecy should be familiar with the last seven years or "Daniel's 70th Week." This is what Jesus is telling us to understand. This final week was not fulfilled in the first century—it literally could not have been. It is yet to come. In Daniel nine, God lays out the master timeline for the first and the second coming of Jesus the Messiah. This timeline of events center around Jerusalem and the Temple. In the middle of these seven years is the "Abomination of Desolation," the great sign for which Jesus is telling us to prepare. But He was far from finished with this topic. In His visit to the Apostle John at least five decades after the Resurrection, Jesus gave a full detailing of this final seven year period in the Book of Revelation. In chapter 12 of that great prophecy, we see a sweeping view of history and future events presented as one continuous flow. Reinforcing the message from the Gospels, we are told not only will Israel flee to the mountains, but we are also told what will happen when they arrive. A detailed breakdown on Revelation 12 follows in chapter two of this book.

So if we can accept that, yes, it will happen, this includes accepting that the Jews will have to leave their home in Israel and flee to "the mountains" to survive, this leaves us only one inescapable conclusion: we have much work to do. That is the purpose of this book and we who have contributed to this book pray it resonates in your spirit as it does ours. For reasons that our Father only knows, these things have been largely hidden from the Church for two thousand years.

NEVER AGAIN WILL HAPPEN AGAIN

Hitler's genocidal rampage against the Jews of Europe is rightly looked upon with horror and was basically the event that turned the attention of the world back to Israel and (ironically) gave the nation of Israel new life. There is little doubt there was a powerful supernatural component behind Germany's hatred of the Jewish people; and Hitler did not rise to power in a vacuum. Many agreed with him. Unfortunately, many of the German Church either tacitly or explicitly approved of Hitler's crimes against the Jews. The assent/non-action of the German Catholic Church is well documented, but four hundred years of Protestant conditioning, beginning with "hero" Martin Luther, set the stage for fellow Jew-hater Hitler to rise. As Christians, we must deal with these truths. That's not to say Hitler himself was a Christian nor was his Third Reich a Christian government, but, without Church consent and even participation, Hitler would arguably never have risen to power in the first place.

Combined with the perceptions (true and false) of the Crusades, the Holocaust cemented in the mind of most Jews that Christians were not to be trusted. Certainly Christians could not be counted on to defend the Jews when genocidal maniacs reappeared. It is from the all-too-real ashes of the Holocaust that the term "never again" was born. Never again would the Jewish people leave their defense to others, or be without a homeland to stand in. Never again would a holocaust be permitted, not in Europe or anywhere else. Since 1948, the Jews proudly and defiantly shout "never again" when threatened (see Iran the past few years) and who can blame them? But that's the most tragic element of this drama; the Bible declares that their pride and instance on relying on themselves and not on their God will not provoke His protection, but rather His chastisement. Jacob's Trouble will be the time of unparalleled defeat for Israel, "such as never was since there was a nation until that time" (Daniel 12:1). This plainly means not only will there be another holocaust, but that this holocaust will be even "worse than the first." The Jews ethnic and national nightmare "never again" will indeed happen again. Most of the Church doesn't even realize this is coming. Those who do would mostly prefer to fly away to heaven beforehand. This is an unacceptable and untenable situation.

Now, with new generations growing up with several degrees of separation from World War II, we are witnessing the same demonic hatred boiling to the surface today in post-Christian Europe. Calls for the expulsion and extermination of the Jew are becoming routine. Swastikas are reappearing. The memory of the Holocaust is fading away, and coupled with rising denial that it ever occurred at all, this is the proverbial canary in the coal-mine. And despite assurances from western leaders to the contrary, it is being primarily (though not exclusively) driven by Islam. The hatred of the Jew has a 1,400 year history in Islam and is in fact codified in their holy texts. Once again, the Satanic purpose of this hatred should make this very clear to us—fiery persecution is coming again and Satan's wrath will be squarely on those God has chosen: the Jewish people. As we hopefully can see in Revelation chapter

12 and the Gospel accounts, the land of Israel itself will be ground zero. Sometimes you will hear the unvarnished truth from Muslim leaders like Hezbollah secretary-general Hassan Nasrallah: "if the Jews all gather in Israel, it will save us the trouble of going after them worldwide." God's plan has not changed and neither has Satan's; "never again" will come, and it will come quickly.

Not only is this reality lost on Israel today, but among those who should know better: the Church of her Messiah. He has told us beforehand! Alas, when Jesus first came as suffering servant, those whose commission it was to retain and know the Oracles of God allowed their traditions and wishful thinking to overrule the plain words of their Savior, and so it is once again. This situation is no different today. The future told through the Biblical Prophets is a consistent message, a desperate warning from a Father not just to Israel, but to all the nations who will choose sides at the end of the age before the great and terrible Day of the Lord. Many Christians who I personally know and count as dear friends are utterly blinded by their love for Israel and the "never again" defiance, assuming that since they have survived this long, that God will never allow their land to be invaded again, never allow them to be defeated militarily, or even effectively challenged. That is the very attitude God is going to have to shatter - and indeed, it will take Israel's national power to be "completely shattered" to accomplish His will. Not only will this realization have a crushing impact on the Church, even so far as the complete loss of faith by some, but the time lost will be tragic. Before the darkness of the Great Tribulation comes will be the time to work, to build what does yet exist: those places in the mountains where those Jews who heed the warnings of Scripture will flee.

HOW DO WE GET THERE FROM HERE?

We now live in a generation that has grown up with Israel as an independent nation. As we see unreasonable animosity towards her from every side, including from newly elected representatives in the United States congress, the ancient winds of persecution calling for Israel's destruction are blowing again. Not just from Iran, though Iran is the next step in this prophetic journey, but also from NATO member Turkey, from leaders throughout Africa and Asia, and, increasingly, in Europe. Stunningly, the most consistent support for the Jewish state is now coming from Egypt, the Arabian Peninsula and the Kurds. Once we re-visit, re-examine and re-commit to understanding what God is saying, we can now see the "big picture" of Bible prophecy, and this all starts to make sense.

A quick note on how I personally "got here:" I was born in 1975, so among my earliest memories are gas lines and the beginning of the Iran-Iraq war (as we will see, there is truly "nothing new under the sun"). After my salvation in the third grade, the love of the return of Jesus and the Bible's prophetic nature was firmly planted in my heart by the Holy Spirit. I always was fascinated by the Scriptures even as a young child and when I was 15, sparked by Iraq's invasion of Kuwait and the resulting "Gulf War" I began seeking to understand the books that I loved reading but couldn't really untangle: Revelation and Daniel. Fast-forward through the years of high school, college, marriage, house and children; in November 2012, God basically pulled me aside and said, "you work for Me now." At that point I re-dedicated myself to understanding these things, even if it meant turning all my previous "understanding" on its head. Six months later the ministry called Wings Of The Eagle was born and WingsOfTheEagle.com launched in August 2013. God was clearly leading me in a particular direction but I never heard any "respectable" teacher agree. So God sent two "confirming witnesses" in the books of men named Joel Richardson (Mideast Beast) and Mark Davidson (Daniel Revisited). Those works opened the floodgates of Berean understanding and of a network of Kingdom relationships that continue to this day. I was so honored and humbled when Joel agreed to be interviewed for this book; you will read his significant contributions in subsequent chapters. In many ways, "Flee To The Mountains" has been in the works since 2014, and my first ever visit to Israel in 2017 sealed it.

It is from the perspective of that lifelong journey that I offer the following for your consideration as to how this will all play out. This is a scenario that stays true to the best of my understanding of what God's Word says will happen next. These will be "Breaking News" events to the world in the coming weeks, months and years, but hopefully these events will come as no shock to those of us who know their Bibles.

1. Iran will launch a full-scale invasion of the Middle East. Specifically, Iran will push into the nations of Iraq, Syria, Saudi Arabia and possibly Turkey. Iran will not attack Israel or even attempt to do so. Iran will advance into these

territories and nobody will be willing or able to stop this campaign for a time. The pretext Iran uses may be helping the Kurds, destroying Sunni terrorists, protecting Shia like Assad or Hezbollah or annexing the Saudi oil fields. Iran may be led in this campaign by a man who is hailed as the 12th Imam/Shia Mahdi. The world will be plunged into deep panic. Peace of mind will be taken from us all (gas lines to the extreme) and Islamic terrorism—specifically Hezbollah and IRGC cells around the world—will spread like wildfire.
(Daniel 7:5, Daniel 8:2-4,20, Daniel 11:2, Zechariah 6:2, Revelation 6:4)

2. Turkey will lead a coalition of Sunni nations (Egypt, Jordan, Saudi Arabia, perhaps Pakistan) to fight back against Iran. Turkish dictator Erdogan may well be the very visible head of this counter-attack. Israel will not be involved. Iran will be completely defeated by this Turkish led coalition. The government of Iran and their Mullahs will be overthrown, the IRGC apparatus will be dismantled. Israel will be thankful to this coalition that the Iranians have been stopped. Turkey will then assume de facto control of nearly all Middle Eastern land and oil, and the world will experience severe economic trouble.
(Daniel 7:6, Daniel 8:5-7,21, Daniel 11:3, Zechariah 6:2,6, Revelation 6:5-6)

3. The Turkish leader (potentially Erdogan) will want to rule it all and may even declare himself Caliph over the "proper" Ottoman Caliphate but he will be deposed or killed quickly. Turkey will oversee the re-drawing of the map of the Mideast into four new nations. This geographical quartering may break into something that very

roughly resembles: "New Turkey" to the north, "New Iran" to the east, "New Arabia" to the west and "new Egypt" to the south. There will be dissension and several military confrontations between this new Turkey and new Egypt allied with new Arabia. Eventually a formally unknown leader will emerge from this northern division and subdue and unite them all. As a united Caliphate, 10 leaders of various Islamic nations will act as one and make peace with Israel via a seven year agreement and the issue of Jerusalem will at long last be "settled". The Jews will finally build their new Temple alongside or around the Dome of the Rock on the Temple Mount. The world will formally recognize this resurrected Islamic Empire and its peacemaking leader. Muslims around the world will begin calling him the rightful Caliph – some will even call him the long-awaited Mahdi.
(Isaiah 28:15, Daniel 7:7-8, Daniel 8:8-9,22, Daniel 9:27, Daniel 11:4-23, Zechariah 6:3,6-8, Revelation 6:8, Revelation 13:1-4, Revelation 17)

4. During the first 3.5 years of the agreement, the Caliph will curry favor by dividing up oil riches among the Empire, but Egypt will resist him and want to leave the confederacy. There will be a fierce war between these "kingdoms" of north and south—this is the "kingdom against kingdom" Jesus Christ warned of as a sign of His coming (Isaiah 19)—but as He told us, the end is not yet. This quarter of the earth will be cursed with war, disease and starvation. Egypt will finally be conquered by this King of the North and then the Caliph will turn to Jerusalem as the new seat of his power. 3.5 years after the agreement was made, he will break the deal and invade Israel. The Great Tribulation – the last 3.5 years before the return of Jesus

when two-thirds of the Jews and untold numbers of Christians are killed - will then commence. (Isaiah 19:1-4, Daniel 8:10-12,23-25, Daniel 11:24-31, Ezekiel 38-39, Revelation 13:5-10)

BUT IT IS FAR FROM HOPELESS!

The common objection to this kind of discussion is "doom and gloom" or "I don't want to hear about the end of the world!" We really need to get into our Bibles if we think the return of Jesus and His millennial Kingdom on earth is anything but good. The events that occur with Israel and the nations are to usher Him in. There is a proverbial "baby" born after these "birth pains" end. The King will come to take back what is His. A nation will be born in a day. The Church that has made herself ready will be married to the Bridegroom and administer this perfect kingdom worldwide. Jerusalem will go from war torn and desolated to the shining crown jewel of the earth. The resurrection will occur when all Christians from all time get new bodies that never age, sicken or die.

A proper understanding of the order of events is critical to God, so it needs to be critical to us. In agreement with our gracious Father, empowered by His Holy Spirit let us preach "the full counsel of God" to every nation to save all those who will hear - to expand that eternal Family of God as large as possible before our King comes to reign. The greatest calling of the Church will be during the Great Tribulation/Jacob's Trouble: to shine the brightest when the darkness appears strongest. Jesus is ever faithful; just watch what He will do though the willing.

THIS BOOK IS DIFFERENT

Throughout this book you will read my interviews with some of the foremost thinkers and front-line witnesses in the Church today from both the Western world and the Middle East on this great topic of Jacob's Trouble and our role therein. I not only admire them and their work greatly, but I have been blessed to have become friends with these mighty men of God; their contributions to this work are invaluable. My eternal gratitude is due to author/filmmaker/Missionary Joel Richardson, Pastor/author Jake McCandless, Jewish/Christian theologian Fred London and Messianic Pastor Israel Pochtar.

If you haven't realized it already, some very popular theories are being shown the door in this book. Preterism, a fancy term meaning Bible prophecy has already been fulfilled, is manifestly untrue. It is obvious that our Lord did not return in 70AD and restore the Kingdom to Israel and He is not ruling from Jerusalem today. Even those "partial preterists" who like to play games say that the Abomination of Desolation happened in 70AD. Well, as we just saw demonstrated, that is impossible. On the opposite end of the spectrum is the doctrine of the pre-tribulation rapture. This doctrine is also untrue. This is the idea that the Church will be removed from the earth prior to the last seven years. Some say it will occur before the last 3.5 years, but the error is the same. Jesus would not have wasted His time using so many writers of the New Testament to issue warnings that do not apply to Christians. Our next chapter will expound much further on this. Suffice to say, the Church will be here for the duration until that great and terrible Day of the Lord when He splits the sky and comes in judgment and to make war.

I know the temptation is to "throw the baby out with the bathwater" after decades of bad exegesis ("Left Behind" and its ilk) but a careful study of the Holy Scriptures will show that, indeed, seven years still remain on the clock. This work is in no way claiming to be a new revelation or anything of the sort, only laying out the scriptural case for this "breaking news of tomorrow" and our Christian response to those events. As Paul said, though we understand all mysteries and have all knowledge, without love, we are nothing. Please read the following pages in light of the fact that all of it is out of the deepest love and devotion to our King Jesus Christ, His Church, for His people the Jews, and for His land, Israel.

In chapters four through six we will process the realization of what God is saying. You will see the details of the "What" the "Where" and the "Why." Then, in chapters seven through nine, we will see what has been done up until our present day; our numerous misunderstandings, misapplications and mistrust do not reflect well on us. But there remains some time—hope and a promise that the Body of Christ—at least some of us—will finally understand. But first, it is important to "establish the facts" of this case.

Chapter 2

ESTABLISHING THE FACTS

"I will provoke you to jealousy by those who are not a nation"

Much like in a legal case, I feel it necessary at this point to lay all of the evidence out on the table. Some is personal testimony, some is circumstantial and inferred, some is direct and observable. Frankly, it's one thing to have a certain understanding of the Bible and its prophetic texts, but another to live and walk with other humans whose very souls are hanging in the balance. Absolutely nobody is helped when we ignore reality and act as if nothing is wrong, or as if nothing is going to change. Especially in this post-modern, post-truth world, even agreeing on what is real is not easy, so that's our first step.

JUDGED ON HOW WE RELATE TO ISRAEL

In Matthew 24 and Luke 12 Jesus tells a parable of the conditions right before His return. And He ends it by asking us a question: "Who then is the faithful and wise servant sent to give them food in due season?" The reference is to Genesis 45. There we see Joseph sent ahead of his brothers into a Gentile nation, specifically to ensure the survival of Israel, to "preserve a posterity for them in the earth." The "servant" in that parable is Joseph, the "them" is Israel. Could Jesus be telling us that "Joseph" is the Church in the last days who will feed the Jews who flee? If so, this places a burden of responsibility on us. "To whom much is given, much will be required…"

I asked bestselling author, filmmaker, Missionary and Bible prophecy expert Joel Richardson what his thoughts were about the Church's responsibility towards Israel in the days ahead, and his answer was profound:

Death is the elephant in the room of life. It is a looming inevitable reality for everyone. No one wants to face it or talk about it, but we will all have to face it. Likewise, within the arena of theology, "the time of Jacob's trouble" is the looming elephant in the room. It is clear within Scripture that it is coming. This is one of the most relevant and pressing matters in all of Scripture. Yet very few theologians are actually wrestling through and talking about it.

We need to look at the Scriptures to understand how God relates to Israel. In Joel chapter 3 for example, He says, "what have you against me, oh, Tyre and Sidon on all of the regions of Philistia?" So you could say "Hezbollah, Hamas, what have you against me?" He is talking about the surrounding nations attacking and persecuting his people, Israel, yet He, the Lord takes it personally. He doesn't say, "What have you against my people." He says, "What have you against Me?" Then He says, "if you think you're going to repay Me, I will swiftly and speedily return all that you have done on your own heads." So there is this dynamic throughout the Scriptures where the Lord actually identifies with His people. How we relate to Israel specifically in the last days will very much determine where we stand before Him on the Day of Judgment, when the Messiah returns. He makes it pretty clear in Matthew 25 for example, where Jesus is expounding upon Joel 3, the judgment of the nations. He will judge the nations largely based on how they treated His people Israel in the midst of their time of tribulation.

There's an awful lot of information in the Scriptures concerning our attitude, our posture toward Israel. Overwhelmingly it is to be an attitude of humility; we have a debt of gratitude to Israel. We have a debt of service to the Jewish people because of what Paul clearly lays out in Romans 11, which is: that the only reason that we as the former heathen have had the doors opened to us is because of the fact that God in his sovereignty temporarily hardened Israel. A large part of Israel has been hardened in order that we, the undeserving heathen, can come in. Therefore we are to honor them because of their history, and the promises made to them. Though you could say, "well a lot of Israel today, they're not believers, they're walking often in rebellion to God and are enemies of Christ." That's true, but Paul also says that they are still beloved because of their ongoing calling and election. So Gentiles are called to stand with Israel as a way of showing gratitude to God, to love Israel regardless as to whether they are believers or not.

CALLED TO THE WITNESS STAND

Born and raised in the suburbs of New York City, I have been around Jews my entire life: traditional and reformed, orthodox and non-practicing. Some of my earliest memories are visiting friends of my parents who were Jewish and playing with their children. I recall being in the Cub Scouts and befriending the nicest boy and I think the only one smaller than I was, who happened to be Jewish. All though grade school, high school and college I naturally gravitated towards Jewish kids—I wonder sometimes if they were brought to me for a divine purpose. Either way, this affinity with Jewish children was unconscious and unintentional. In general, I do tend to connect with those from minority backgrounds, being a bit "odd" and "nerdy" myself makes it natural, I suppose. However, now I believe the best way to explain it is a Holy Spirit ministry gifted to me to reach out in friendship to the Jewish people. As school progressed, I became more aware of troubling anti-Jewish slurs and conspiracy theories, and these ugly realities, in equal measure, saddened and angered me.

It was in my college years that I grew especially close with three very different Jewish friends. One was (and is) a happy-go-lucky, life-loving guy, incredibly kind and personable. Even after our college days we would go to his home and he would gleefully play with my young children. Shortly after we became friends, his mother passed away. With her death also passed from his life any outward expression of following God. I believe my friend and God have been "wrestling" ever since her death.

The second friend was someone I really enjoyed having intellectual conversations with. He was a reader and a deep thinker, and no topic was out of bounds. Even though raised in a Jewish home, he had decided that all religions were equally wrong and he was now an atheist (or agnostic depending on the day). His atheism and my Christianity led us through some exceedingly intense debates over the years. Unfortunately, we aren't close any longer because of disagreements over a few choice subjects, but these things happen. However, one thing that really sticks with me was the ring that he always wore on his hand: a large lion's head. I asked him about it once. He said he didn't know of any significance other than that it was a family gift. As I explained about the lion representing the tribe of Judah (and Jesus being the ultimate Lion of Judah) he actually contemplated his Jewishness for a moment and the prospect that this man Jesus was a Jew Himself. Though the moment was fleeting, it was profound, at least to me.

The third friend was a young lady. We started dating while I was in college but she still a senior in high school (yikes). Over those very "interesting" two+ years we talked about marriage and starting a family, topics that were not perceived as odd because though both her parents were Jewish, they had divorced and her mother remarried a Gentile Christian like me. Granted I didn't see any real religious observances, and they made it a point not to have inter-faith contention. But one time I did attend a family Passover Seder at her uncle's home and they were all blown away by the fact that I actually knew what Passover was and why they celebrated it. I had the dual conundrum of realizing that most Jews thought Christians had no clue about Passover and that yes, most Christians likely had no clue about it or anything else Jewish. Also of great value to me was seeing first hand some bigotry and latent hatred from both sides; some in her family were not happy I was not Jewish, and some in my family were not happy that she was. In the end, thanks mostly to me, it didn't work out and we had the kind of break-up where you basically never speak again. HOWEVER, I found out later that the Gospel seed I had cast had taken root and blossomed by the Spirit and she is now a Christian! I'm pretty sure I know what made an impact and prepared her heart; let's just say we should never be afraid to use the book of Revelation to witness.

So it is on this "witness stand" I can affirm that my love of the Jewish people is not just theoretical or even purely motivated from any sense of obligation towards a scriptural mandate. There is no guilt involved. I have loved them as people for as long as I can recall—and as I learned later in life, they are a very special people to God. Now as an adult in the ministry of the Church, of course I have dear Jewish friends, many of whom follow the same Messiah as I do, and that fills me with unquenchable joy and hope. One day, after all that is coming, there will be those who will choose Him as their King, and His reign over them and over all Israel as a nation will be everlasting. However, we all know that today, there is a very small minority of Jews who know and profess Jesus, and so there are some hard truths that will now be introduced into evidence.

THE COLD, HARD FACTS

Today, for the first time since 70AD, there are more Jews living in the land of Israel than outside of her. This trend will only accelerate because God is the trendsetter. Now this is not to say that the present return of the Jews to the land is the final return spoken of in the Bible, and it is not to say that this present return will bring God's unswerving favor and protection to the land. Both assertions are categorically false. Trust me, I know of the heated and sometimes fellowship-rending debates that this has caused especially among the Messianic Jews in Israel today. I was moderating a panel discussion at a conference in 2018 about "Jacob's Trouble" and the Messianic Jewish leader who had flown into the middle of the USA from Israel to take part in it literally left the building when it was time to discuss. We had to get a last minute replacement from the audience. Thankfully this brother was more than up to the challenge, being a prolific Christian author and blogger. The reality of a future time of Trouble for Israel is frankly seen as "bad for business" by our Brothers in Christ - this is a cold, hard fact. Yet it remains true: the Jews are coming back to Israel and they will be facing invasion and defeat when Gog of Magog (the Antichrist) rises and makes then breaks the covenant of peace with them.

What of the vast majority of the Jews both today and in the future? The fact is that unsaved Jews are not and will not be reading the New Testament. In the parlance of my generation, "duh." Many Jews in Israel today are extremely secular and agnostic; they aren't even reading the Old Testament, much less the New. So how on earth are they going to recognize the fulfillment of Daniel nine when their leaders sign the "covenant with Death and Sheol" and the breaking of it half way through when the invasion comes? Words matter. Jesus said what He said for a reason. He said it to the Church so we might warn them ("duh" again). So what's the problem? Unfortunately, there is a popular teaching that has sprung up that says Jesus is pulling a fast one on us. Yup, that's right. Putting aside the obvious falsehoods of Replacement Theology

(God is done with the Jews forever) and Preterism (this prophecy was already fulfilled in 70AD) there is a newer teaching (aka an excuse) created to "gloss over" the problem of Jesus telling the Church what to do: "He was saying it to the Jews." The Lord is doing a "bait and switch" you see...these prophetic warnings only apply to the Jews because the Church will obviously be raptured to Heaven well before the Abomination of Desolation. This is head-shaking on so many levels it is difficult to articulate a rebuttal. I have been told "the Gospel of Matthew is just for the Jews." Huh? Even if one accepts this lunacy, what about Mark and Luke when the say the exact same thing? And why is only Matthew 24 for the Jews? What about four chapters later (mere weeks after the prophecy was told to the apostles) when the same people in the same location are told by the same Man: "Go therefore and make disciples of all the nations, baptizing them in the name of the Father and of the Son and of the Holy Spirit, teaching them to observe all things that I have commanded you; and behold, I am with you always, even to the end of the age." Is this Great Commission just for the Jews? Of course not, that would be absurd. And so is the belief that Jesus warning about the Abomination and Israel fleeing to the mountains is "not for the Church." If you are one who holds to this terrible teaching, I say sorry, not sorry to burst that bubble. News flash: God has a plan to deliver the Good News of the Messiah to Israel. It's the same plan in effect for 2,000 years now. See Romans 10: "How then shall they call on Him in whom they have not believed? And how shall they believe in Him of whom they have not heard? And how shall they hear without a preacher? And how shall they preach unless they are sent?" God will get the word to them the same way He always has since Messiah came: the Church (Christ in us) will be their one and only hope of hearing the warning. Let me repeat this for emphasis: God will not - I dare say cannot - deliver this Gospel message without the Church, because that's the way He chose to ordain things to work. We will go deeper into this awkward and often painful topic in chapter seven.

Now, once we as the Church see the truth of the matter, some more practical "cold hard facts" should begin to emerge in our minds. These Jews, at least in this specific part of Israel, (at present over 700,000 people) will need to be told by us: 1. TO go, 2. WHEN specifically to go, and 3. WHERE specifically to go. In Chapters four through six we will break each of those issues down into more specifics, but basically, this will require detailed planning and building a network of people and a physical infrastructure beforehand to handle such a great weight of souls. Time is not our friend.

FINALLY UNDERSTANDING REVELATION 12

I am utterly convinced the master key to accepting these facts is the proper exegesis of Revelation chapter 12. My personal education by the Holy Spirit on this passage began 20 years ago with just one phrase ringing in my spirit making me restless: "wings of the great eagle." I believe if we re-examine this chapter with fresh eyes, this text can become so clear that every Christian can just "get it," and subsequently "get to work" being about our Father's business, right up until His return. Perhaps we haven't arrived there yet because re-examination would potentially contradict long-held traditional teachings? At the core, this chapter splits the last seven years of this age into two equal halves:

First Half: "the woman fled into the wilderness, where she has a place prepared by God, that they should feed her there one thousand two hundred and sixty days."

Second Half: "the woman was given two wings of a great eagle, that she might fly into the wilderness to her place, where she is nourished for a time and times and half a time, from the presence of the serpent."

But there is so much more than that. Really, this is the entire history of the Bible and the war between God and Satan from Genesis through the Great Tribulation, in one chapter. From the ancient past to the last days of this age, let's break down Revelation 12 verse by verse:

The Past

<u>The Woman, Israel - in pain to bring forth Messiah - the story of the Old Testament</u>

> *A great sign appeared in heaven: a woman clothed with the sun, and the moon under her feet, and on her head a crown of twelve stars; and she was with child; and she cried out, being in labor and in pain to give birth (Revelation 12:1-2).*

So why does the Woman = Israel? The sun, moon and 12 Stars is a reference to Genesis 37:9-10 -

> Now he (Joseph) had still another dream, and related it to his brothers, and said, "Lo, I have had still another dream; and behold, the sun and the moon and eleven stars were bowing down to me." He related it to his father (Jacob) and to his brothers; and his father rebuked him and said to him, "what is this dream that you have had? Shall I and your mother and your brothers actually come to bow ourselves down before you to the ground?"

The crown means she is royalty, which is also alluded to in Genesis. God's plan to marry His bride is a consistent theme throughout the Bible. The Old Testament tells us the "where" (land of Israel/Jerusalem), the New Testament tells us the "who" (all believers in Messiah, Jew and Gentile). Ok. So we have this Woman, and she is pregnant. The child she is in pain to deliver is clearly the Messiah, Jesus, as later verses reveal.

The Red Dragon, Satan – his career

> Then another sign appeared in heaven: and behold, a great red dragon having seven heads and ten horns, and on his heads were seven diadems. And his tail swept away a third of the stars of heaven and threw them to the earth. And the dragon stood before the woman who was about to give birth, so that when she gave birth he might devour her child (Revelation 12:3-4).

Spoiler Alert: the Dragon is Satan (as we will confirm in a few verses). Satan's career is long and well documented. We know from Isaiah 14, Ezekiel 28 and his temptation of

Jesus in the desert, that he has great beauty, wisdom, cunning and political power. When he offered Jesus "all the kingdoms of the world", he meant it. It is why Satan is called "ruler of this world" by Jesus and "god of this world" by Paul. His title of "prince of the power of the air" reveals his current status in heaven over his fallen angels called the "principalities" or "gods" of the nations. (Read Daniel 10 for a look behind the curtain of the principalities of Iran and Turkey, for example). It is only Israel that does not have a Satanic "principality" over her, that is the responsibility of Michael the archangel (Daniel 12:1). That struggle between Satan and Michael is a critical point to remember as we go though Revelation 12. So starting with man's fall in Eden, we see that Satan legally acquired nearly every national government/empire on earth aside from Israel. The heads, horns and crowns signify this international control.

The well-known "Beast with seven heads and ten horns" of Revelation 13 and 17 cannot be properly understood without Revelation 12:3. The seven heads are seven geographic kingdoms that Satan directly controls throughout history and the goal of each is the destruction of Israel and her Messiah. It is not a coincidence that the dream of Joseph was just referenced in Revelation 12:1-2, as the story of Joseph's life marks the start of Israel being subject to the cruel dominion of the first of those seven Satanic empires. Joseph was sent as a slave to Egypt and all his nation was soon to follow. Egypt was the first head.

Now, let us turn our attention to the 1/3 of the stars of heaven. Those stars are angels – see Job 38:7: "when the morning stars sang together and all the sons of God shouted for joy." Also see Job chapters 1 and 2 where are they also called "sons of God" and Satan is there among them. Why is this important? It is important because there is documentation of the angels (sons of God) coming to the earth in Genesis 6:2-4. Yes, I've heard all the theories on that "controversial" chapter but, to me, nothing fits either the narrow or wider context aside from angels themselves coming to the earth. Plus, 2 Peter 2:4 and Jude 6 unapologetically support this literal interpretation, so I'm very comfortable there.

With the Dragon standing before the Woman to devour her Child, we fast forward from Genesis all the way through to the Gospels. We go from Egypt, the first Satanic kingdom/head, all the way though the times of Assyria, Babylon, Persia and Javan to the sixth, Rome. For it was under Roman rule that Herod gave the order to kill all male children to end the Messiah's human life as soon as it began.

As an interesting side note, "Israel's birth pains" happen at two different points of history, both culminating in Jesus the Messiah on earth. See Isaiah 66:6-9:

> *A voice of uproar from the city, a voice from the temple, The voice of the LORD who is rendering recompense to His enemies. Before she travailed, she brought forth; before her pain came, she gave birth to a boy. Who has heard such a thing?*
>
> *Who has seen such things? Can a land be born in one day? Can a nation be brought forth all at once? As soon as Zion travailed, she also brought*

forth her sons. Shall I bring to the point of birth and not give delivery?" says the LORD. "Or shall I who gives delivery shut the womb?" says your God.

Some say this "land born in a day" refers to Israel in 1948, I don't agree. BEFORE her pain came (the final birth pains of her Trouble), she gave birth to a boy. This is the male child of Revelation 12, Jesus the Christ. Then come the birth pains and the "sons," who are her children. We will read about them in a few verses. The day here is the Day of the Lord, when the Kingdom of Jesus will be set up. Take heart, it will happen, regardless of what Satan attempts to do to try and stop it.

<u>The Male Child, Messiah, ending Daniel's first 69 Weeks</u>

And she gave birth to a son, a male child, who is to rule all the nations with a rod of iron; and her child was caught up to God and to His throne (Revelation 12:5).

Some Bible scholars and teachers claim this son who will rule the nations with a rod of iron, who is currently in heaven at God's throne, is not Jesus. This claim has no exegetical basis. See Revelation 2:27, 19:15 and Psalm 2:9 for clear confirmation of this Son's identity. The one and only interpretation of this verse is the birth, death and resurrection of Jesus Christ. Another element we can't miss here is something that is critical to our timeline, namely the prophet Daniel and his famous 70 Weeks concerning Jerusalem (Daniel 9). The prophecy began with Jeremiah as the kingdom/head of Babylon invaded and took Judah captive. In studying that particular scripture, Daniel was told that when Jerusalem was rebuilt, the "countdown" would begin, and 70 periods of seven years would remain until this age ends. Well, those periods of seven ("weeks") began under the fourth kingdom/head, Persia. Daniel was told directly that the killing of Messiah would mean the 69th week was over and only the 70th remained. As we see here, this Son Jesus was indeed born and after completing His earthly ministry, He was taken to heaven where He remains waiting for the final seven years to end.

The Present

THIS IS WHERE WE ARE TODAY: we are currently living between the 69th and 70th weeks of Daniel. We exist in the space between Revelation 12:5 and 12:6, in the precious time when the Kingdom of God is now opened to all of the Gentile nations. Whosoever will believe in that Son of God, the Light being brought from Israel to the Gentiles and become the one new man in Messiah, the Church. There is a time lapse ordained by God for the Gospel to go forth between the glorious resurrection of Jesus and the "confirming of the covenant," the event that begins the final seven-year countdown. The final week begins when the "prince to come" – the leader of the final Satanic empire/head – makes an agreement of peace with Israel; I strongly believe this must involve Jerusalem and the Temple Mount. When it does occur in the not-too-distant future, verse six of Revelation 12 will commence:

The Future

First half of Daniel's 70th Week – Beginning of the birth pains

> *Then the woman fled into the wilderness where she had a place prepared by God, so that there she would be nourished for one thousand two hundred and sixty days (Revelation 12:6).*

For some reason, this verse is where most folks begin to get tripped up. They assume it is talking about the LAST 3.5 years. Why? If seven years are yet to come, why leave the first half out of this otherwise comprehensive narrative? Note the very obvious lack of Satanic pursuit of the Woman. Also note the terms in which the 3.5 years are stated (1,260 days). This is not the place for a full study of the "birth pains" Jesus tells us to watch for as a sign of His return, but realizing He was referring to Isaiah 19:1-4 when He says, "kingdom against kingdom" is huge. It connects the Olivet Discourse in Matthew 24/Mark 13/Luke 21 to Isaiah 19 to Daniel 11. The short version is: the birth pains begin with the kingdom against kingdom wars between Egypt and Israel's northern neighbors Turkey/Syria/Iraq; and there is a place in between those warring nations that seems to remain neutral: Jordan and Arabia. (For a full breakdown of this and many other subjects related to the end times, please see my full online Bible course at EndTimesForBeginners.com).

To dig down a bit further, the biggest obstacles most Christians have in understanding Revelation 12:6 are twofold: the timing of it, and the people involved.

The Timing: In context, this is what happens after the 69th week of Daniel - the 70th. Most every Bible student knows this "week" is a seven-year period divided into two equal halves of 3.5 years. So after the events of the 69th, we must start the 70th and the first 3.5 years obviously happen first. Yet most readers just leapfrog right over that first half and say this is the latter half. There is no justification for that in the text or in the context or even in simple logic. As we will see down in verse 13, those last 3.5 years are detailed quite clearly and with an obvious time reference to boot. Quite plainly, this is describing the first 3.5 years, what Jesus called the "beginning of sorrows" or "birth pains." The "covenant with Death and Sheol" between Israel and the surrounding Islamic nations is what kicks off the 70th week. That is the critical event we must be watching for.

The People: since this is post-resurrection, is this verse referring to the people of physical Israel (the Jews) or all Christians (per Romans 9)? First, the symbology must remain consistent. If the Woman is physical Israel in verses 1-5, she still represents physical Israel in verse six. Also, the geographic markers are strong enough, both here and in related scriptures, to say it is referring to events in and around the LAND - the nation-state of Israel in the Middle East. So the "fleeing" and the "wilderness" must be localized around Israel proper.

What is this wilderness? "Wilderness" = "erēmos"; empty landscape, or desert. So what is going on that would necessitate Israel (Jews and/or Christians) being nourished in the nearby desert? The time of "wars and rumors of wars" and "kingdom against kingdom" has now arrived;

the kingdoms around Israel will be at war with each other for control. Specifically, Daniel 11 and Isaiah 19 reveal that the kingdom to the north of Israel (Turkey/Syria/Iraq) will be fighting the kingdom to her south (Egypt). The in-between nations of Jordan and Saudi Arabia may well declare neutrality and allow Jews and Christians to have safe haven there for these initial 3.5 years. Some would say this "place prepared by God" is in a totally different nation, but that will be addressed later in chapter 8 of this book. So the first 3.5 years, instead of being leapfrogged over, are shown to be a critically important time. The Church would do well to pray on this.

The Archangel Michael, war in Heaven at midpoint

> And there was war in heaven, Michael and his angels waging war with the dragon. The dragon and his angels waged war, and they were not strong enough, and there was no longer a place found for them in heaven. And the great dragon was thrown down, the serpent of old who is called the devil and Satan, who deceives the whole world; he was thrown down to the earth, and his angels were thrown down with him. Then I heard a loud voice in heaven, saying, "Now the salvation, and the power, and the kingdom of our God and the authority of His Christ have come, for the accuser of our brethren has been thrown down, he who accuses them before our God day and night. And they overcame him because of the blood of the Lamb and because of the word of their testimony, and they did not love their life even when faced with death. For this reason, rejoice, O

heavens and you who dwell in them. Woe to the earth and the sea, because the devil has come down to you, having great wrath, knowing that he has only a short time" (Revelation 12:7-12).

The implications of realizing this is a future event, not a past one, is mind blowing I know; it changes one's whole paradigm. We have been taught Satan has already been cast from heaven to earth, that he "knows his time is short"...but how can "short" mean 2,000+ years? Unfortunately, erroneous theological traditions have overtaken the Word of God in this area. We must break free. This is in heaven, either during or at the end of the first 3.5 years. It is impossible that this is talking about pre-70th week, impossible that it is talking about pre-resurrection times. In the narrative of the story, the Dragon has already finished trying to kill the Child, and he lost that battle as we just saw. This is a new war and it has yet to begin. Notice that this war involves two complete sets of angelic armies facing off, rather than a "one on one" between Satan and Jesus. The text does not say who started the war, but per Daniel 12:1, Michael "rises" and then the "time of trouble" begins. It is no coincidence that the Antichrist's invasion of Jerusalem immediately follows this heavenly eviction. In fact, it's really the only way it can occur.

In Daniel 10:21, Michael the "chief prince," i.e. archangel, is called the "withholder" against evil angelic principalities. This is who Paul was referring to in 2 Thessalonians 2:7 - the one who "withholds" the lawless one until his time arrives. Michael is therefore revealed as "the Restrainer." Daniel 8:10 says the Little Horn had power into the heavens and caused angels to fall to the earth, so the timeline here is firmly established via multiple scriptures. The casting out of Satan and his army from heaven is a future event.

And as I mentioned earlier, if there was any real mystery, it is revealed that the Dragon in this story is Satan. Also that he was the Serpent in the Garden of Eden. These two descriptions will be utilized again in upcoming verses for specific reasons. Is Satan accusing you before God right now? Then he's still in heaven. After he is cast out, he will have no ability to accuse anyone! He literally has no audience with God to do so (see Zechariah 3:1).

This is what I call the "bright side" to the last 3.5 years - the great outpouring of the Holy Spirit to those on earth will be unprecedented in history. This will be when the Spirit is poured out on all flesh (Joel 2:28-32). For the first time, there will be no Satanic hindrance in the "second heaven"; no more Satanic army continually attempting to come between God and earth. The signs and wonders through the Church at that time will be unspeakably awesome. How do we overcome him when he arrives? By being willing to be martyred for Jesus. Pray that you don't love your life so much that you cannot remain faithful if He calls you to lay it down.

Now at this point of the story, and only now, we have come to the "short time." What is the short time exactly? It is 3.5 years as we will see. As Satan will be enraged about his eviction, he will lash out in wrath. In other words, the Great Tribulation that Jesus told us is coming will thus begin. We must accept that **the Great Tribulation is Sa-**

tan's Wrath against the Church and Israel, it is NOT God's Wrath against the world.

The final 3.5 years – the Great Tribulation

> *And when the dragon saw that he was thrown down to the earth, he persecuted the woman who gave birth to the male child. But the two wings of the great eagle were given to the woman, so that she could fly into the wilderness to her place, where she was nourished for a time and times and half a time, from the presence of the serpent. And the serpent poured water like a river out of his mouth after the woman, so that he might cause her to be swept away with the flood. But the earth helped the woman, and the earth opened its mouth and drank up the river which the dragon poured out of his mouth. So the dragon was enraged with the woman, and went off to make war with the rest of her children, who keep the commandments of God and hold to the testimony of Jesus. And the dragon stood on the sand of the seashore (Revelation 12:13-18).*

As we have seen, the Woman who gave birth to Messiah is physical Israel. She represents the Jewish people. What else do we know happens at the midpoint of these 7 years? The Abomination of Desolation. That moment when the "covenant" is broken and Jerusalem is invaded, the one called Antichrist is revealed as he sits in the rebuilt Temple and declares that the God of the Bible is defeated. The Great Tribulation begins with the purging of the Jews from Judea, exactly as Jesus said and the prophet Zechariah describes in Zechariah 13:8-9 and 14:1-2. But, as always, God ensures a remnant survives. The namesake of my ministry "Wings Of The Eagle" comes from this verse. Exactly what these wings are and where this place is, is what this book is all about. Our Father is described as a great eagle several times, specifically regarding keeping Israel alive in the (Arabian) wilderness during the Exodus. God will protect this remnant. Notice how this 3.5 year time period is worded: "time and times and half a time," the exact same way as Daniel 7:25 and 12:7 describe the timeframe of the Great Tribulation. This is intentional and meant to draw a distinction between this verse and verse 6 earlier. They are not the same 3.5 years. Notice too that Satan has changed names from the Dragon to the Serpent. The "Dragon" is power and authority and strength, the king of brutality and hate. The "Serpent" on the other hand is subtle, shining, ear-tickling: the great deceiver.

This water from the Serpent's mouth is fascinating to me. It sounds as if perhaps Satan is trying to get revenge for Noah's flood. It could be literally from his mouth, referring directly to his words, or a proclamation or new law. It would "sound good." Perhaps it could take the form of an offer to "resettle" the Jews outside of the Middle East. Or, it could be an actual flood of water supernaturally ordered by him that the physical earth actually swallows up before it reaches those fleeing Jews. At any rate, if this chapter is teaching us anything, it is to interpret the symbols presented accurately. The "earth" may well be a symbol also, and it may well be representing the Church. The bottom line is, he is unable to kill all the Jews like he has always wanted to do via his seven kingdoms. He now has resurrected the final one, making it "the eighth and of the seven," the one "whose deadly wound was healed" (Revelation 13:3, 17:11)–the Islamic Caliphate. Unable to finish the job against physical Israel, he turns to eradicate the rest of God's people, the Church. Who are these "children of Israel" who keep the commandments of God and testify of Jesus? They are Christians. Romans 8:29 reveals that Jesus is the "firstborn among many brethren;" He said Himself that in Matthew 12: "For whoever does the will of My Father who is in Heaven, he is My brother and sister and mother." This will be the time we, as His Church, must prepare for most of all. There will be no harder time in history to be a Christian. I see countless thousands, maybe even millions, of martyrs during these last 3.5 years.

The question we all must contend with is, will the pressure of the Tribulation get to us and will we deny Him with a sword on our necks; or on the necks of our loved ones? Will physical or emotional suffering cause us to lose faith? This is how the Great Apostasy happens. Satan and his Caliphate will try to convert or kill every single Christian. He will get close but a remnant again will remain; then our King will return to avenge our blood and overturn every kingdom and government on earth. The Day of the Lord will be great and terrible indeed.

On the final verse of the chapter (12:18), most translations have this as verse one of chapter 13. The reason for this is the word "histēmi" which means "was standing." Who is the one standing on the seashore witnessing the Beast kingdom rising in its final form? Was it John who was shown the vision or the Dragon as the uninterrupted narrative continues? Personally, I would put it here at the end of chapter 12 because it does seem to be Satan who is about to implement his plan to eradicate God's people once and for all. We are told in Revelation 2:13 that Satan's throne is in Pergamum near the Turkish coast, so it makes sense that he would go there at least to start operations. Revelation 13 does seem to be a direct continuation of this story, where we are told exactly what nations comprise the Beast kingdom and how exactly the worship of Satan is enforced during the last 3.5 years. But alas, that is outside the scope of this book…

ISRAEL PROVOKED TO JEALOUSY BY SOME FOOLISH GENTILE CHRISTIANS

Hopefully at this point we can see what the Word of God is laying out for us. That He will be utilizing His Church, as foolish as some of us are at times (#GuiltyAsCharged). We can even begin to see into God's master plan from the BEGINNING for Israel, and for all mankind. Plan A is still plan A, and we can have a part in it. To be sure, "Jacob's Trouble" will be the most painful time in the history of the Jewish people, and the world as a whole, but if we can see our Father's great purposes in it, we are freed to step into our destiny as fearless proclaimers of the Good News. Yes, the King of Israel is coming. Repent, therefore, and receive salvation.

> *They have provoked Me to jealousy by what is not God; they have moved Me to anger by their foolish idols. But I will provoke them to jealousy by those who are not a nation; I will move them to anger by a foolish nation (Deuteronomy 32:21).*

I say then, have they stumbled that they should fall? Certainly not! But through their fall, **to provoke them to jealousy, salvation has come to the Gentiles**. *Now if their fall is riches for the world, and their failure riches for the Gentiles, how much more their fullness! For I speak to you Gentiles; inasmuch as I am an apostle to the Gentiles, I magnify my ministry, if by any means I may provoke to jealousy those who are my flesh and save some of them. For if their being cast away is the reconciling of the world,* **what will their acceptance be but life from the dead?** *(Romans 11:11-15)*

Direct from the Word of God, we are told the Resurrection of the Dead directly coincides with Israel's acceptance of their Messiah, Yeshua (Jesus). It is that Great and Terrible Day of the Lord towards which all of these momentous events lead. And indeed, all Israel will at that time be saved. Are we now ready for the rest of the Biblical evidence?

Chapter 3

ISRAEL FLEEING TO THE MOUNTAINS THROUGHOUT THE BIBLE

"Surely the Lord God does nothing, unless He reveals His secret to His servants the prophets"

As someone active in inter-denominational ministry, one of my great joys is seeing the Father create divine connections between His people. Over the past 10 years I have gotten to know many diverse Pastors and Church leaders (some more visible, some under the world's radar) and am just so very thankful for a glimpse into their heart of devotion to, and love for, our Lord Jesus. I have witnessed some being promoted in the Kingdom for what seemed to be one overriding quality: being teachable.

REMAINING TEACHABLE

In recent years, I have made a concerted effort with the Pastors I have sat under to just watch and learn from them; their knowledge of the Word, their habits in studying it, and its application in their day to day lives. I know I have a long way to go in Christ-likeness and the willingness to be continuously taught has been a tremendous help and blessing. I have also discovered that, sometimes, what God wants to work on through our teachability is our theology. I've been turned around on several Scriptural issues–sometimes completely around–and have accepted that it is ok to admit it publicly. "Things I have been wrong about" is likely not something we want to see on a Pastor's resume but I made a full video about that very thing recently and am in the midst of filming a documentary on one specific area of Scripture I was greatly mistaken about. In the end, I think it is very healthy and glorifies the Holy Spirit as our true teacher.

Pastor Jake McCandless is on a similar course. As soon as I saw his book, Spiritual Prepper in early 2017, I knew the Lord was in it. I hadn't read it yet, mind you, just had seen the title and cover. So I followed him on Twitter, saw him interviewed on Joel Richardson's "The Underground," and later that year during the inaugural "Understanding the Times" conference in Tyler, Texas he came up and introduced himself to me. We had an instant connection and his passion for the Church was obvious. THEN I read his book. Turns out he is a "classically reared" Southern Baptist who has been undergoing bold refinery in his own theology. It was what launched Spiritual Prepper and his new life's work appealing to the Church in the West, "Stand Firm Ministries." Before we get to the many Scriptural examples of Israel fleeing to the mountains, I wanted to share with you the questions I asked Pastor Jake in an effort to show where remaining teachable can lead.

I asked, "As a pastor educated in the traditional Southern Baptist roadmap, how have your views changed on the end times generally and Jacob's Trouble specifically?"

I don't know if you could say I'm on the traditional roadmap because there's probably a low percentage who do have seminary degrees. But I did go to a traditional Baptist Bible College and Baptist Seminary. I have pastored in two different Baptist denominations and led a lay seminary for our association.

In my undergrad, all of my professors would have been textbook dispensational premillennialists. So, in theology class that system was taught. But there was a solid teaching on interpreting the Bible.

In seminary, it varied from teacher to teacher. But my Revelation professor in seminary was an amillennialist, who viewed everything as symbolic. This was very impactful on me. At the time I began to lean towards the symbolic view. Also I was planning on pursuing a PHD at the time and teach seminary. And it was completely uncool or unacademic to be premillennialist. There was lots of pressure from seminary peers to not be "simple-minded."

So, from my undergrad I was a dispensational pre-mill, pre-tribber, and then for a few months I was not necessarily an amillennialist, but I was deeply influenced by the symbolic view. My roots in hermeneutics caused me to struggle going full amillennialist because Revelation 20 clearly presented a millennial kingdom.

The impact of that seminary professor caused me to downplay prophecy and the end times. Also, the emphasis on exegetical study and expository preaching also caused me to downplay the end times.

Seven years out of seminary a friend of mine kept pushing me to consider some prophetic aspects. So, I began watching YouTube videos. Most were political conspiracy type stuff, but I began to sense something was going on. Then I became captivated by the "forgotten" prophecies, those that talked about the state of Christians at the end of the age like Matthew 24:10. It was in studying that I just began to realize how precisely we needed to receive prophecy. Through what at the time seemed like a fluke schedule problem I took a course in seminary on "Theological Interpretation of Scripture." I can't even define this view. But it basically is Scripture interpreting Scripture. These principles created in me an intense conviction to let Scripture speak for itself. This helped me isolate Scripture from preconceived ideas.

With that foundation, I taught an Old Testament Survey Seminary Class. In that, the text book was organized by the covenants. I became overwhelmed to the significance of the covenants. And therefore, the Abrahamic and Davidic Covenant called for a Millennial Kingdom. I left that semester of teaching completely convinced that the only possible Biblical view was premillennialism. As I began to consider how the Old Testament covenants called for the Millennial Kingdom, I also began to realize how that the dispensational view was new with shaky roots. So, I began to lean towards classical premillennialism, but still had a *hard time abandoning a pre-trib rapture because all the preachers I followed and listened to preached it.*

The first held view to fall for me was the identity and origin of the Antichrist. All I had ever heard was a Revived Roman Empire view of Daniel 2 and therefore a revived European Roman Empire was the only conclusion. But I was on my way to teach through Daniel in the second semester of Old Testament Survey when it hit me that proponents of the Revived Roman Empire view would say that the two legs proved that the final empire was Rome because Rome was split between the East and West. And as I was walking to class, it hit me that the Eastern division of Rome far outlasted the Western division. I wondered why we do not consider the Eastern division.

Then, following class, I went to a late night hospital visit and I was listening to Michael Savage and he had Walid Shoebat on his program. Walid walked through Revelation 17:9-11 which in my opinion is the lynchpin to prove Rome is not the final empire and that it is the Ottoman Empire. I also then realized even books that supported a European Roman Empire as the final empire would talk about the origin of the Antichrist coming from the Middle East. It was at this point I read Islamic Antichrist and Mideast Beast and my mind was settled.

This prepared me for the fact that other trusted views might be wrong. The next to fall was a pre-trib rapture. My professor had opened my mind to the role suffering plays in the lives of believers. This opened a doorway to consider that suffering during the Tribulation time might not be the condemnation we were told we'd avoid by being in Christ. When Spiritual Prepper came out a lady reached out to me on Twitter, Annette Bell, and she walked me through verses about the timing of the rapture. It was clear that it was a "late" timing rapture. Then I studied the pre-trib support verses and found them completely lacking. Again, Scripture spoke for itself.

Next, would be my understanding of the Great Tribulation/Time of Jacobs Trouble. I was asked to participate in a panel on the subject at a big conference. I knew nothing. So, for two weeks I crammed. My eyes were opened to understanding that this current return of Israel was not the "final" return. Then out of the blue a lady contacted me to share about some verses with me. For two hours she walked me through verses explaining what you are writing in this book. And as I walked through the text myself, I realized it speaks for itself.

"What motivated you to create your teaching resource 'Church, we must get Israel right?'"

The Lord! You know I can't even trace the roots of this study. As you study Scripture you see that God has a plan for Israel and for the most part the church is clueless to this. Even churches who are "pro-Israel" don't understand the church's relationship with Israel, the importance of the covenants, the future of Israel, and the role the church will play.

The first time I taught it, the two-session seminar fell on deaf ears. The second time I was to preach it, I had to drive 5 hours. My wife and I talked the whole 5 hours about it. I kept telling her, I'm so convicted that this mes-

sage is one of the most important messages, and it was so vital for the church to hear it. But I couldn't articulate why it mattered to the church so much. How did it affect them now? How was it relevant? We concluded that the few "righteous among us" who preserved Jews during the Holocaust and stood for them had someone along the way set them straight on God's plan for Israel and their relationship with the church. So that was what we were doing; laying a foundation for this generation and hopefully the generation to come.

I asked, "In your view what is the current state of the Church in terms of preparation for the challenges ahead in light of Matthew 24:10?"

The western church—especially the American church—are sheep heading to slaughter. We aren't remaining faithful now with just daily challenges in the most comfortable and luxurious society in history. We don't even know that Christians can suffer. We don't have a clue what Scripture tells us about the end times. And few are truly walking in the Spirit. So, when the ultimate deception that leads to turning away comes which is the Antichrist and False Prophet carrying out Islamic Eschatology of their Mahdi and their Jesus. This will pull the rug out from "professed believers" and they are going to question everything and be suckered into turning away.

I asked, "What should American Christians be doing right now as we witness this exponential rise in antisemitism and anti-Israeli propaganda from all realms of our culture?"

Ultimately, antisemitism is demonic. It defies logic. It sneaks in the hearts and mouths of people who if they really thought about it wouldn't practice it. But we're blinded. I believe American Christians need to be informed to the relationship they have with Israel. They need to come to understand that we're grafted into Israel. The language of spiritual Israel, ethnic Israel, national Israel, etc needs to be thrown out of Christian lingo. It's vital that we inform American Christians of the truth of the relationship, the covenants, and the future of Israel. So maybe they don't get sucked into antisemitism. Of course, more needs to be done, but if this not done, nothing else will be.

Finally, I asked: "Why should American Christians care about Jews in Israel? Today or in the days before Jesus returns?"

Because we're Israel. Not that we replace them or that we're a spiritual Israel. But Jesus is the Jewish Messiah, the Jewish King. We have joined them. And for Scripture to be true, Israel has to be redeemed. We have to see ourselves as them. We need to love and be compassionate and heartbroken for them as we would for any people group, but I believe a step more so because they are God's people and we have been adopted into their family. Also we know that Israel is ground zero for Satan's attacks.

BY THE MOUTH OF 34 WITNESSES

So now we come to the evidence directly from the Word of God. Jesus has not introduced a new concept in this critical passage "(let the reader understand) then let those who are in Judea flee to the mountains" (Mark

13:14). The reader is told to "understand" because the message was already in the Bible. Not just about the Abomination of Desolation coming to Jerusalem from the book of Daniel, but the consequence of that event. It is written all over the Old Testament, and even walked out by Paul in Galatians 1 and included as a central theme in the book of Revelation as we saw in our last chapter. What you are about to read is this same theme, presented over and over again in the Holy Scriptures: by the halfway point of the last seven years at the latest, the Jews in and around Jerusalem, and the greater nation, will have to leave the country to avoid genocide and enslavement.

As God tells us the principle in Amos 3:7, He always reveals the future to His servants the prophets before it happens. He makes sure to do it, as He is not a God of confusion. And deception will be everywhere in the last days, growing more and more until the Day that Jesus returns. We need to know what He has already said to avoid being deceived! It's either God's Word or our own understanding. Choose wisely. As a safeguard, He has also promised us from the very beginning that, "by the mouth of two or three witnesses every word may be established." So even though there are far more than "two or three" passages of Scripture that establish the word (as you will see there are more like 34), I do see three distinct categories over the 1,600 years of Old Testament history:

1. ABRAHAM'S DAY

Genesis 14:10-11–"5 Kings of Israel/Jordan" in Dead Sea Valley escaping "4 Kings of Iraq/Iran/Turkey":

> *Now the Valley of Siddim was full of asphalt pits; and the kings of Sodom and Gomorrah fled; some fell there, and the remainder fled to the mountains. Then they took all the goods of Sodom and Gomorrah, and all their provisions, and went their way.*

Genesis 19:17–Lot and family in Sodom (in or very near Jordan):

> *The angel said, "Escape for your life! Do not look behind you nor stay anywhere in the plain. "<u>Escape to the mountains, lest you be destroyed.</u>"*

NOTE: Moab and Ammon are born there

2. THE TRIBES

Genesis 45:7–Joseph in Egypt, in the middle of the 7 year famine:

> *God sent me before you to preserve a posterity for you in the earth, and to save your lives by a great deliverance.*

Exodus 15:12-13–Moses led Israel across Red Sea into Midian/Arabia/NEOM - the earth helped the woman:

> *You stretched out Your right hand; The earth swallowed them. You in Your mercy have led forth*

the people whom You have redeemed; You have guided them in Your strength To Your holy habitation.

Deuteronomy 32:21, 43—Moses song on the Last Days:

<u>I will provoke them to jealousy by those who are not a nation; I will move them to anger by a foolish nation.</u> [Gentile Christians]...Rejoice, O Gentiles, with His people; For He will avenge the blood of His servants, And render vengeance to His adversaries; He will provide atonement for His land and His people.

Judges 6:1-2: land of Midian, 7 years, in the mountains:

Then the children of Israel did evil in the sight of the LORD. So the LORD delivered them into the hand of Midian for <u>seven years</u>, and the hand of Midian prevailed against Israel. <u>Because of the Midianites, the children of Israel made for themselves the dens, the caves, and the strongholds which are in the mountains.</u>

3. THE PROPHETS

1 Kings 19/Galatians—the path of both Elijah and Paul. From Sinai in Arabia (NEOM) through the Mountains/Wilderness of Edom, Moab and Ammon to Damascus then to Jerusalem:

> From Judah…he went a day's journey <u>into the wilderness</u>…an angel touched him, and said to him, "Arise and eat"…and he went <u>in the strength of that food</u> forty days and forty nights as far as <u>Horeb, the mountain of God</u>. (1 Kings 19:3-8)

> <u>I went to Arabia</u>, and returned again to Damascus…Then <u>after three years</u> I went up to Jerusalem (Galatians 1:17-18)

2 Kings 8:1-5—the prophet sends "the woman" out of the land to avoid a seven year famine:

> Then Elisha spoke to the woman whose son he had restored to life, saying, <u>"arise and go, you and your household, and stay wherever you can; for the LORD has called for a famine, and furthermore, it will come upon the land for seven years.</u>" So the woman arose and did according to the saying of the man of God, and she went with her household and dwelt in the land of the Philistines seven years. It came to pass, at the end of seven years, that the woman returned from the land of the Philistines; and <u>she went to make an appeal to the king for her house and for her land</u>.

Psalm 55:6-8—wings to escape into the wilderness:

> So I said, "<u>Oh, that I had wings</u> like a dove! I would fly away and be at rest. Indeed, I would wander far off, <u>and remain in the wilderness. Selah. I would hasten my escape from the windy storm and tempest.</u>"

Isaiah 16:1-4—the Lamb sent into the wilderness of Moab to hide the outcasts:

> *Send the lamb to the ruler of the land, from Sela to the wilderness, to the mount of the daughter of Zion.* For it shall be as a wandering bird thrown out of the nest; so shall be the daughters of Moab at the fords of the Arnon. Take counsel, execute judgment; make your shadow like the night in the middle of the day; *hide the outcasts, do not betray him who escapes. Let My outcasts dwell with you, O Moab; be a shelter to them from the face of the spoiler.* For the extortioner is at an end, devastation ceases, The oppressors are consumed out of the land.

Isaiah 21:1-5—preparing a table in the "wilderness of the sea" for the labor pains:

> The burden against the Wilderness of the Sea. As whirlwinds in the South pass through, so it comes from the desert, from a terrible land. Therefore my loins are filled with pain; *Pangs have taken hold of me, like the pangs of a woman in labor…prepare the table, set a watchman in the tower, eat and drink.* Arise, you princes, anoint the shield!

Isaiah 21:11-15—where the Watchmen will be watching from:

> The burden against Dumah [Edom/NEOM]. He calls to me out of Seir, "watchman, what of the

night? Watchman, what of the night?" The watchman said, "The morning comes, and also the night. If you will inquire, inquire; return! Come back!" The burden against Arabia. <u>In the forest in Arabia you will lodge</u>, O you traveling companies of Dedanites. O inhabitants of the land of Tema, bring water to him who is thirsty; <u>with their bread they met him who fled. For they fled from the swords, from the drawn sword, From the bent bow, and from the distress of war.</u>

Isaiah 26:16-18–Labor Pains, Israel seeking God in their Trouble/chastisement:

<u>LORD, in trouble they have visited You, they poured out a prayer when Your chastening was upon them. As a woman with child Is in pain and cries out in her pangs, when she draws near the time of her delivery</u>, so have we been in Your sight, O LORD. We have been with child, we have been in pain; we have, as it were, brought forth wind; we have not accomplished any deliverance in the earth, nor have the inhabitants of the world fallen.

Isaiah 37:30-32–the 3+ year rule of the Assyrian:

This shall be a sign to you: You shall eat <u>this year</u> such as grows of itself, and the <u>second year</u> what springs from the same; also in the <u>third year</u> sow and reap, plant vineyards and eat the fruit of them…<u>And the remnant who have escaped of the house of Judah</u> shall again take root downward, and bear fruit upward. <u>For out of Jerusalem shall</u>

> go a remnant, and those who escape from Mount Zion. The zeal of the LORD of hosts will do this.

Isaiah 40:1-5–the message of end-time Elijah(s) during the 7 years - the King is Coming:

> "Comfort, yes, comfort My people!" Says your God. "Speak comfort to Jerusalem, and cry out to her, that her warfare is ended, that her iniquity is pardoned; for she has received from the LORD's hand double for all her sins." The voice of one crying in the wilderness: "prepare the way of the LORD; Make straight in the desert a highway for our God. Every valley shall be exalted and every mountain and hill brought low; the crooked places shall be made straight and the rough places smooth; the glory of the LORD shall be revealed, and all flesh shall see it together; for the mouth of the LORD has spoken."

Isaiah 52:6-8–the Church preaches to Jews under the Beast - and the unity it brings:

> Therefore My people shall know My name; Therefore they shall know in that day that I am He who speaks: 'Behold, it is I.' How beautiful upon the mountains are the feet of him who brings good news [Gospel] Who proclaims peace, who brings glad tidings of good things, who proclaims salvation [Yeshua]. Who says to Zion, "Your God reigns!" Your watchmen shall lift up their voices, with their voices they shall sing together; for they

shall see eye to eye when the LORD brings back Zion.

Isaiah 59:19-20—the flood from Satan's mouth:

When the enemy comes in like a flood, the Spirit of the LORD will lift up a standard against him."The Redeemer will come to Zion, and to those who turn from transgression in Jacob," says the LORD.

Isaiah 66:14-15—context of the woman in labor pains/Jacob's Trouble:

The hand of the LORD shall be known to His servants, and His indignation to His enemies. For behold, the LORD will come with fire and with His chariots, like a whirlwind, to render His anger with fury, and His rebuke with flames of fire.

Jeremiah 4, foreshadowing the Church's role:
Verses 5-6 = The first 3.5 years the Church warning Israel to flee:

Declare in Judah and proclaim in Jerusalem, and say: "blow the trumpet in the land; cry, 'gather together,' and say, 'assemble yourselves, and let us go into the fortified cities.' Set up the standard toward Zion. Take refuge! Do not delay! For I will bring disaster from the north, and great destruction."

Verses 7-13 = Midpoint: Breaking of their 7 year covenant and the invasion of Judea by armies of the Desolator, Antichrist:

> The lion has come up from his thicket, and <u>the destroyer of nations is on his way. He has gone forth from his place to make your land desolate.</u> Your cities will be laid waste, without inhabitant. For this, clothe yourself with sackcloth, lament and wail. For the fierce anger of the LORD has not turned back from us. "And it shall come to pass in that day," says the LORD, "that the heart of the king shall perish, and the heart of the princes; the priests shall be astonished, and the prophets shall wonder." Then I said, "Ah, Lord GOD! <u>Surely You have greatly deceived this people and Jerusalem, saying, 'you shall have peace,' whereas the sword reaches to the heart.</u>" <u>At that time it will be said to this people and to Jerusalem, "A dry wind of the desolate heights blows in the wilderness toward the daughter of My people--not to fan or to cleanse--a wind too strong for these will come for Me; now I will also speak judgment against them</u>. Behold, he shall come up like clouds, and his chariots like a whirlwind. His horses are swifter than eagles. Woe to us, for we are plundered!"

Verses 14-31 = Last 3.5 years, the Great Tribulation/Jacob's Trouble and the Gentile Christians are witnessing locally:

> "<u>Make mention to the nations, yes, proclaim against Jerusalem, that watchers come from a far</u>

country and raise their voice against the cities of Judah. The whole city shall flee from the noise of the horsemen and bowmen. They shall go into thickets and climb up on the rocks. Every city shall be forsaken, and not a man shall dwell in it. *For I have heard a voice as of a woman in labor,* the anguish as of her who brings forth her first child, the voice of the daughter of Zion bewailing herself; she spreads her hands, saying, 'woe is me now, for my soul is weary because of murderers!'

Jeremiah 9:1-2—the lodging place for refugees fleeing Israel:

Oh, that my head were waters, and my eyes a fountain of tears, that I might weep day and night for the slain of the daughter of my people! *Oh, that I had in the wilderness a lodging place for travelers;* that I might leave my people, and go from them!

Jeremiah 31:2—Israel running from Antichrist's invasion into the wilderness:

The people who survived the sword found grace in the wilderness—Israel, when I went to give him rest.

Jeremiah 48:9, 40-41—wings of the eagle in land of Moab, the woman in labor:

"*Give wings to Moab,* that she may flee and get away; for her cities shall be desolate, without any to dwell in them. Therefore behold, the days are

> coming," says the LORD, "that I shall send him wine-workers who will tip him over and empty his vessels and break the bottles...for thus says the LORD: "Behold, one <u>shall fly like an eagle, and spread his wings over Moab</u>. Kerioth is taken, and the strongholds are surprised; the mighty men's hearts in Moab on that day shall be like the heart of a <u>woman in birth pangs</u>.

Ezekiel 7:5-7, 16-18—Jacob's Trouble, survivors of Israel escape to the mountains:

> A disaster, a singular disaster; <u>behold, it has come! An end has come, the end has come; it has dawned for you; behold, it has come! Doom has come to you, you who dwell in the land; the time has come, a day of trouble is near</u>, and not of rejoicing in the mountains...<u>Those who survive will escape and be on the mountains</u> like doves of the valleys, all of them mourning, each for his iniquity. Every hand will be feeble, and every knee will be as weak as water. They will also be girded with sackcloth; horror will cover them; shame will be on every face, baldness on all their heads.

Ezekiel 14:22—the remnant brought out of Jerusalem:

> Yet behold, there shall be left in it <u>a remnant who will be brought out, both sons and daughters; surely they will come out to you</u>, and you will see their ways and their doings. <u>Then you will be comforted concerning the disaster that I have</u>

> brought upon Jerusalem, all that I have brought upon it.

Ezekiel 20:34-36—Jesus will reveal Himself to Israel though the Church:

> And I will bring you into the wilderness of the peoples, and there I will plead My case with you face to face. Just as I pleaded My case with your fathers in the wilderness of the land of Egypt, so I will plead My case with you," says the Lord GOD.

Daniel 1:5—3 years training so Israel can serve King Jesus:

> And the king appointed for them a daily provision of the king's delicacies and of the wine which he drank, and three years of training for them, so that at the end of that time they might serve before the king.

Daniel 11:32-35—the Church providing the final martyr witness to the Jews:

> The people who know their God shall be strong, and carry out great exploits. And those of the people who understand shall instruct many; yet for many days they shall fall by sword and flame, by captivity and plundering. Now when they fall, they shall be aided with a little help; but many shall join with them by intrigue. And some of those of understanding shall fall, to refine them, purify them, and make them white, until the time of the end; because it is still for the appointed time.

Daniel 11:41—the "mountains" of Jordan are protected from Antichrist:

> He shall also enter the Glorious Land, and many countries shall be overthrown; but <u>these shall escape from his hand: Edom, Moab, and the prominent people of Ammon</u>.

Daniel 12:3—eternal rewards for the Church who does this work:

> Those who are wise shall shine like the brightness of the firmament, and those who turn many to righteousness like the stars forever and ever.

Hosea 2:14-15—the same wilderness of Midian/NEOM and Jordan as in the days of old:

> Therefore, behold, <u>I will allure her, and bring her into the wilderness, and speak tenderly to her</u>. And there I will give her her vineyards and make the Valley of Achor a door of hope. And there she shall answer as in the days of her youth, <u>as at the time when she came out of the land of Egypt</u>.

Micah 2:12-13—remnant of Israel assembled then Jesus comes to rescue them and bring them back into the Land:

> "I will surely assemble all of you, O Jacob, <u>I will surely gather the remnant of Israel; I will put them together like sheep of the fold [Bozrah]</u> like a flock

in the midst of their pasture; They shall make a loud noise because of so many people."
   THEN
"The one who breaks open will come up before them; they will break out, pass through the gate, And go out by it; their king will pass before them, with the LORD at their head."

Micah 5:3-4, 7-8—remnant of Israel being fed in the nearby gentile nations:

> <u>Therefore He shall give them up, until the time that she who is in labor has given birth; Then the remnant of His brethren shall return to the children of Israel</u>. *And He shall stand and feed His flock in the strength of the LORD, in the majesty of the name of the LORD his God; and they shall abide, for now He shall be great to the ends of the earth...then the remnant of Jacob shall be in the midst of many peoples, like dew from the LORD, like showers on the grass, that tarry for no man nor wait for the sons of men.* <u>And the remnant of Jacob shall be among the Gentiles, in the midst of many peoples.</u>

Zechariah 13:8-9—one third will escape the Antichrist's invasion and be fed the Gospel:

> *"And it shall come to pass in all the land,"* says the LORD, *"that two-thirds in it shall be cut off and die,* <u>but one-third shall be left in it: will bring the one-third through the fire, will refine them as silver is refined, and test them as gold is tested. They will</u>

<u>call on My name</u>, *and I will answer them. I will say, 'this is My people'; and each one will say, 'The LORD is my God.'"*

Malachi 4:2-5 - gentile priests teaching Israel about their Messiah before the Day of the Lord. Wings of the eagle, Horeb/Sinai, end time Elijah's mission:

> *<u>But to you who fear My name The Sun of Righteousness shall arise with healing in His wings</u>; And you shall go out and grow fat like stall-fed calves... Remember the Law of Moses, my servant, which I commanded him in <u>Horeb</u> for all Israel, with the statutes and judgments. Behold, I will send you Elijah the prophet before the coming of the great and dreadful Day of the LORD.*

BREATHE

Now you may want to pause and prayerfully process the Realization of what God is saying to us...to you. In the next 3 chapters, we will dive into the details of our response to the Call. These are details that may have never before been published simply because no one thought it necessary: the "What" the "Where" and the "How."

PART 2: REALIZATIONS

Chapter 4

REALIZATION: THE WHAT

"The people who know their God shall be strong, and carry out great exploits. And those of the people who understand shall instruct many"

What exactly is it that we are to do then? If the Church will be here for Daniel's 70th week, we will have work to do. Must it commence even now? As we saw in Scripture, that work will include "feeding" the Jews who flee Israel before the Antichrist invades. Then, during the last 3.5 years –the Great Tribulation/Jacob's Trouble–this feeding will take the forms of both natural food and the Gospel of their Messiah, Jesus.

THE PURPOSE OF END TIME PROPHECY

Ultimately, all Bible prophecy is about Jesus Christ and His testimony (Rev. 19:10). As in the original Church at the outpouring of the Holy Spirit in Acts 2, seeing prophecy fulfilled can result in thousands of souls being saved all at once. Generally, this is what God wills to accomplish with the prophetic Scriptures - to glorify Himself and save as many people as possible from hell. Part of the ministry of the Holy Spirit is to tell us, the Church, "things to come" (John 16:13). But, as we have been detailing, there is an overarching drama playing out with the Jews and the land of Israel in the center and the city of Jerusalem at the heart. In that respect, the purpose of all this end time stuff is simply to lead Israel to their Messiah, back to life from the dead.

In other words, the basic purpose of end time prophecy is to "know what Israel ought to do." Inherent in that is not only preaching Jesus to them generally, but the whole *specific* process of warning them of the covenant with the Beast, warning them to flee to the mountains when the invasion arrives, preparing said mountains in the months and years prior to accommodate many thousands of Jews, and there tell them that Messiah is coming, and oh so quickly.

MEN WHO UNDERSTOOD THE TIMES, TO KNOW WHAT ISRAEL OUGHT TO DO

In 1 Chronicles 12:32 we told of "the sons of Issachar who had understanding of the times, to know what Israel ought to do." Prophetically, this is tied to Daniel 11 where the prophet tells us of "the people who know their God shall be strong, and carry out great exploits. And those of the people who understand shall instruct many." Those exploits and those instructions, I am convinced, are about Israel being preserved during the final seven years of the age. Clearly in our own strength these things are not possible— we explore that further in Chapter 7—but with our God, all things are possible.

In the course of the past few years of getting to know Saints from around the world, the Lord connected me to a Brother named Fred London. Fred is a Jewish man who now follows Jesus as Lord (the same goes for his formally Orthodox Jewish wife). For years he has toiled within the Church to bring the looming time of Jacob's Trouble and the Christian's role in it to the surface; mostly finding this message falling upon deaf ears. It is my hope that by including his laboring in this book, the message will reach those who need to hear it the most. He graciously agreed to answer my questions extensively and so I include them here.

I asked "What does the Scripture say the Church's role in the Great Tribulation/Jacob's Trouble is exactly? What about the first 3.5 years?"

If we fail to become the Church as she was intended to be in our present days, we will be ill-prepared to be the Church required in the end-times, to be God's faithful witness on earth to the Jews, the nations, and to the "rulers and authorities in heavenly places."

I believe the word to the American Church in this hour could be summed up in the scripture, "For it is time for judgment to begin with the household of God"—a judgment that must first begin individually. And, since we know, or should know from Scripture, that the unsaved Jew will be unprepared for what is looming on the horizon and referred to in Scripture as "The Time of Jacob's Trouble," it is incumbent upon the Church to be prepared, not only theologically, but in true spiritual maturity, and not only for her own sake, but for the sake of the Jew, and ultimately, for the sake of God's Testimony to His faithfulness to the Everlasting Covenant according to the Eternal Purpose.

In Jeremiah Chapter 30, where it makes reference to Israel in the latter days, it says, "All your lovers have forsaken you, they do not seek you." Notice the term, "lovers" is used. In a very short time, all nations will prove to have been just that—mere lovers. We can already see nations once friendly to Israel, not merely turning their backs on her, but directly turning on her, and the dominos, what's left of them, are going to continue to fall.

So, if all the nations have forsaken her in the time of her greatest national crisis, who does that leave to be that "friend who sticks closer than a brother?" The Church! Soon, the Church will be the only friend Israel has left on earth. This is the ultimate end-time calling and purpose of the Church. The combination of prophetic Scripture, along with Jewish, Church, and World Histories convinces me that, in the future, God will be calling the "True" Church to be as a Corrie Ten-Boom family, the Dietrich Bonhoeffers, the Oskar Schindlers, and countless other lesser known unsung heroes.

I say, the "True Church," because the issue of Israel and the Jew in the midst of the nations will be the ultimate "litmus test" in revealing the "True Church." Just as "not all Israel, is Israel, it will be revealed that not all the professing church is the "True Church." A sentimental, romanticized, soulish love for Israel, along with a fascination for all things Jewish, will not be able to withstand what the

Church will be called upon to do. It will require something more than planting a tree in Israel. Only a Divine love by the Spirit will be able to withstand the risk and self-sacrifice, perhaps even the ultimate sacrifice, on behalf of the Jews in that day.

I am reminded of one of the most moving and gut-wrenching scenes I have ever witnessed, which came in the final scene of the movie, "Schindler's List." That German Gentile, who saved so many, repeatedly bemoans in a self-inflicted torment, "I could have gotten more out!" "I could have gotten more out!" At the conclusion of that scene we see the Jewish response of overflowing gratitude for what Schindler had done for them. The spokesman from the Jewish survivors attempts to reassure him that he could not have done more.

And, in the midst of the anguish of his soul, they surround and embrace him, extending comfort in return for his labors, sacrifices and risks on their behalf. How prophetic is that? Years later, Schindler would be honored by the Jewish people as being formally recognized as a "Righteous Gentile." Today, you will find his grave located in Jerusalem, the only former Nazi to be granted such an honor. What if we are faced with the same sort of rejection and disappointment as Martin Luther experienced when things didn't go as expected and the Jews don't respond in droves to the gospel of their Messiah? If this "pillar of the faith" who started out with the sincere intention of blessing the Jew, only to wind up cursing the Jew towards the end of his life, is it possible that we are capable of responding in similar fashion? If we don't see things from God's perspective, you bet we are!

This should serve as a sober warning to each one of us, that should we fail to "guard our hearts with all diligence" and fail to continually "pay close attention to ourselves and to our teaching," there is a potential "Martin Luther" lurking inside each one of us. There is a day soon coming, and in many ways, already is, when being a professing "lover of the Jews" and "lover of Israel," will no longer be in vogue. It will be increasingly risky and costly.

Just as Shadrach, Meshach and Abed-nego represent a type of corporate Israel, as they were cast into the "fiery furnace," will that "fourth man," which I believe can also be applied to representing the Body of Christ, be willing to enter that "fiery furnace" with them? Remember what Thomas said with the best of intentions in response to Jesus foretelling what would befall Him in Jerusalem? "Let us also go, so that we may die with Him." Well, we know how that turned out. As Jesus was being arrested, Thomas, along with the rest of the disciples severed himself from that commitment about as quickly as Peter severed that poor slave's ear.

In the final analysis, how much of a difference might the Church have made had she made a more concerted effort to raise a greater public alarm and mobilize in more practical ways to save as many Jews as possible? Considering all of the major obstacles involved, maybe not significantly. But, the real issue is as Jesus said, "Woe to the world because of its stumbling blocks! For it is inevitable that stumbling blocks come; but woe to that man through whom the stumbling block comes."

In Matthew 25, where Jesus foretells of the judgment, we see a direct correlation between how the nations or the Gentiles treated His Jewish brethren during their times of greatest need, and resulting in how they were ultimately judged. It is not that loving the Jew somehow earns us a ticket to heaven. But, it does bear witness to the authenticity of our love for God. The following verses are but small samplings I will cite in order to reinforce my points: Luke 15:31: "And he said to him, 'Son (Church), you have always been with me, and all that is mine is yours. But we had to celebrate and rejoice, for this brother of yours was dead and has begun to live, and was lost and has been found.'" Romans 15:26-27 - "For Macedonia and Achaia have been pleased to make a contribution for the poor among the saints in Jerusalem. Yes, they were pleased to do so, and they are indebted to them. For if the Gentiles have shared in their spiritual things, they are indebted to minister to them also in material things."

It's why Jesus could say, "to the extent that you did it to one of these brothers of Mine, even the least of them, you did it to Me." And, by the same token, "As you did it not to the least of these brothers of Mine, you did it not to Me." In other words, we show our love for Christ in the way in which we tangibly demonstrate that love to His Jewish brethren. Proverbs 24:11-12 - "Deliver those who are being taken away to death, and those who are staggering to slaughter, oh hold them back. If you say, "See, we did not know this," does He not consider it who weighs the hearts? And does He not know it who keeps your soul? And will He not render to man according to his work?"

How reminiscent is that of the empty claims of ignorance by so many German citizens, who witnessed the cattle cars filled with Jews as they headed toward the death camps, and could see and even smell the continuous billowing of smoke coming out from the crematorium chimneys. Even beyond the sights and smells, there were the perpetual rumors of the atrocities being spread far and wide through word of mouth.

2500 years ago, a Moabitess named Ruth made this remarkable statement to a Jewess named Naomi, a statement which the Jew will need to hear and see demonstrated by the Church in that day when the Jew will need her the most. "For where you go, I will go, and where you lodge, I will lodge. Your people shall be my people, and your God, my God. Where you die, I will die, and there I will be buried. Thus may the Lord do to me, and worse, if anything but death parts you and me." Ruth got it! And, God saw fit to record the story of this, otherwise, simple woman in the Bible for all time. Why? So that the Church of the future would also "get it!"

Mordecai had this sobering counsel for Esther when her people were faced with annihilation, and the Church would do well to take it to heart. "Do not imagine that you in the king's palace can escape any more than all the Jews. For if you remain silent at this time, relief and deliverance will arise for the Jews from another place and you and your father's house will perish. And who knows whether you have not attained royalty for such a time as this?"

So, what does this mean for the Church? Just as the full identity of Jesus was revealed to the Roman centurion as He hung before him on the Cross, so too, will Jesus be revealed to the Jew as they see the Church willing to endure the Cross for the sake of His brethren. It is for this very reason that the Church must be made aware and prepare for the days ahead when Israel and the Jew scattered abroad will need her the most.

It has been said that the best thing you can do for a future spouse, even before you know who that might be, is to become strong in your faith. Likewise, the best thing the Church can do for the Jewish People in preparation for the difficult times that are yet to come when they will need her the most, is to become corporately strong in the faith, and functioning as God originally intended, "that she might serve the purposes of God in her generation."

If the Church isn't what she's supposed to be in the present, she will have a very difficult time in being what she will be required to be in the future. The Scriptures tell us that prior to Christ's return, it will be the most perilous time in World History, and especially for Jews and Christians. But, they also tell us, that, for the Church, it will be the time of her greatest glory and ministry leading to the salvation of the Jewish People, that remnant of Israel, called according to the promise of the Everlasting Covenant.

We see the theological mandate encapsulated in Romans Chapter 11. I use the term, "encapsulated," because this one chapter truly represents the sum total of Scripture *concerning God's Everlasting Covenant with Israel and what God intends that to mean for the Church, in theology, attitude, practice and overall responsibility. In Israel's welfare is the Church's welfare, with their destinies inextricably linked, that apart from the remnant of Israel, the Church "should not be made perfect."*

Isaiah 35:3-4 - (The Church) Encourage the exhausted, and strengthen the feeble. (God is addressing a third party here). Say to those with anxious heart, "Take courage, fear not. Behold, your God will come with vengeance; the recompense of God will come, but He will save you."

The issue of Israel is the issue of the Church and the issue of Israel is the issue of the nations. To be the corporate Body of Israel's Messiah, willing to lay her life down for the sake of His brethren's redemption, is the ultimate calling and purpose of the Church at the end of this age. Jesus said, "Salvation is of the Jews" and He is calling upon the Church to return the favor.

As to the first 3 1/2 years of the 70th Week of Daniel, although, not much is specifically written relative to that time it is no less critical, and arguably more so in that it will greatly determine how the Church will respond during the last 3 1/2 years. Despite the fact that there are differing views as to what will prophetically signal the last 7 years time clock, from a conservative standpoint, this is my sense from what I glean from the Scriptures. There will be a formal peace agreement between Israel and many nations historically hostile to Israel.

A man will emerge from a country that is not among the larger players in the region. This man may not be the author of what will result in a perceived state of "peace and security" but may broker it or at least solidify this agreement between Israel and its neighbors, which may very well be recognized by other countries around the world. I also take literally that a Third Temple will be rebuilt and the daily sacrifices re-instituted as a result of this peace agreement. It is apparent to me that during this time this relatively brief season of "peace and safety" will lead to a false sense of security, having "trusted in the arm of flesh," and therefore, with their guard down, will have become "a land of unwalled villages."

These conditions, which historically, would never have led to a false sense of security by Israel will ultimately be exploited whereby Israel will be caught napping, so to speak, and suddenly be attacked by multiple nations resulting in an invasion, a devastating defeat of the Israeli Army, a wholesale expulsion from The Land, with many of the Jews living in Israel being captured or killed, with the real prize being that of the City of Jerusalem, where the prophetic "abomination of desolation" is fulfilled by the Antichrist.

This monumental event will mark the end of the first 3 1/2 years of the 70th Week of Daniel and the beginning of the final 3 1/2 years, also, referred to as "The Great Tribulation" and "The Time of Jacob's Trouble." But, during the first 3 1/2 years, "those who have insight will give understanding to the many." They will take advantage of the freedom that they have during this time of relative peace so that, as Jesus said, "So, you too, when you SEE all these things, recognize that He is near, right at the door." It will exponentially compel "those with insight" to plant eschatological seeds among unbelieving Jews, many of whom will "take these things to heart" and will have had "brought to their remembrance" during "The Time of Jacob's Trouble."

And so, the necessary preparation and spreading of this prophetic message will be stepped up and greatly intensified by the Church ("those with insight") during the first 3 1/2 years. Ideally, the Church will have already been preparing long before this most crucial of times, so that they, in so many words, can "hit the floor running." If not, as Jesus warned in reference to this future time, you are likely to have a situation, where, "If a blind man (the Church) guides a blind man (the Jew), both will fall into a pit." And, since the Church has been given much, much will be required of her, and that, without excuse.

I asked "As a Jew in America, how do you see your personal role during Jacob's Trouble?"

My focus is primarily in seeing this vital message taken to the Church in making her aware of the calling and purpose that God has commissioned her to fulfill during this most perilous of times, when the Jew will need her the most. And so, for the present, I believe that this is my indirect personal role in preparing the Church for her most critical future role, "The Time of Jacob's Trouble."

Realistically, especially as a Jew, without Divine intervention, it is quite difficult to presume to have any particular role aside from an ultimate life and death witness. If I should still be alive at "The Time of Jacob's Trouble" being *considered both a Christian and a Jew, my life will be in double jeopardy leaving the choice of whether I am persecuted and likely martyred for being one or the other to my persecutors. And so, due to the times in which we live, coupled with my age, my sense of urgency is focused on the here and now. But, what's most important is "to serve the purpose of God in my generation" in whatever capacity he has called me to.*

I asked, "How does the current state of global antisemitism compare to 1930's Europe?"

Let me begin by stating that there is a spiritual dynamic at play as described in the Bible, which is the most critical aspect needing to be understood, beginning with Evangelicals. Although, there is certainly a fair amount of commonality found between the current state of global antisemitism as compared to 1930's Europe, there are two major factors that now play a rather significant part since the end of World War II and the Holocaust, not only politically, but far more importantly, eschatologically. They are the establishment of the state of Israel in 1948 and the spread and impact of Islam in recent years, especially, in Europe, where in recent years, there has been an unprecedented in-flow of Muslims throughout the continent.

We already see the political and social impact of this inflow, or invasion, if you will. We see the immediate impact that two Muslim freshmen representatives are having in the United States Congress. I cannot help but call to mind the words of Jesus, "When you see these things..." True! This is only one piece of the bigger prophetic picture, but quite significant, nevertheless.

In this hi-tech world among civilized society, anti-Semitic and anti-Israel propaganda knows no limits in its speed and efficiency in distribution, both in the written and spoken word. In addition to that, as the saying goes, "A picture is worth a thousand words" and those who spew forth their anti-Semitic positions take full advantage of images that place Israel in the worst possible light.

Throw in the general ignorance of World History and it is no wonder that you have a situation where country after country, once friendly to Israel, even those who for her statehood in 1948, have been turning against Israel. And, as alluded to earlier, the dominoes are going to continue to fall until only the True Church will emerge and remain as a friend to Israel, even at the risk of paying the ultimate price of that friendship. Why? Because they know what is at stake.

They understand their calling and responsibility to be that "vessel, fit for the Master's use," that they might "serve the purpose of God in their generation"– that purpose of being something of a midwife in assisting the Great Physician in bringing forth that "nation born in a day."

I asked, "What are the most dangerous false teachings in the Church today regarding Israel and the Jews?

Two of the most prominent and long accepted teachings by a large portion of the Evangelical Church in America: the belief in an imminent pre-tribulation rapture and the belief that the re-establishment of the state of Israel signaled the prophecies fulfillment of the Final Return of the

Jewish People back to the Land. Although, not always, these two end-time views are quite often found to be taught and believed as being "two sides of the same coin."

On their face, these two end-time views seem relatively harmless despite their adherence to sound doctrine, and that is precisely what makes them so potentially dangerous, and this is what I want to address to some extent. What I want to say may not be in the tidiest form due to it being within the format of an interview, but they will be thoughts, or rather, convictions that I have held for many years, and in which, I have continued to examine and re-examine over those many years.

Some may find some of what is expressed hard to swallow, and yet, swallow they will! Others will simply and unfortunately choke on what is expressed, and ultimately, spit it out. And, for those who have the spiritual tenacity to roll it around in your mouth for a while, even in this, you are exhibiting a refreshing example of being a true Bearer. Circumstances do not permit me to cite the scores of Scriptural passages which have led me to the views I hold and for the examination of others, but very much welcome the opportunity to do so at another time.

If you look back at all the false prophets in Scripture, there was one common thread found among them above all others in their messages: "Peace! Peace! When there is no peace!" "Surely, this shall not happen to you!" "Peace and Safety!" It's no wonder that these types were always popular and in great demand, that is, until "sudden destruction" came upon them!

This is essentially the message that has been dominating the Church in America and much of the Messianic Jewish community in Israel for quite some time. It is the belief of an imminent rapture on the one hand, and a belief that the re-establishment of the state of Israel in 1948 was the fulfillment of prophecy, and marked the beginning of the Final Return of the Jewish People back to the Land, never to be uprooted, again. They will "live in quiet and at ease, and no one will make them afraid."

Now, if you know without a shadow of doubt that God has called you to a work in Israel and even to make aliyah—for those who may not be familiar with that term, it essentially means to "go up" or to emigrate to Israel—then, after much prayer and having counted the cost, if you still have that same burning passion to go, then, you should go.

But, this wholesale recruitment of Jews being told that they need to return to the Land for no other reason than that they are Jews, and that it will be an arc of safety for them, then, I consider that to be based upon a false premise. Now, if you know what lies ahead, really know what lies ahead according to the objective reading of Scripture, then, I would consider that as legitimately having counted the cost. Otherwise, it could prove to be disastrous. Either, you pay now, or you're liable to pay later.

Now, I'm not suggesting that any of these people are false prophets or false teachers in the sense that they are false brethren. But, what I am suggesting is the possibility that perhaps many have applied the Method of Wishful Thinking in their approach to Biblical interpretation. There's no doubt in my mind that present-day Israel represents a most critical step in the restoration process, but in light of what I read consistently throughout the Scriptures, although, I wish it were not so, present-day Israel does not meet the last days criteria for the Final Return, which God has set forth.

I want to suggest to you that getting it wrong on one or both of these issues, and quite often, they're found joined together, is not a matter of mere difference of opinion. Rather, I believe that the consequences for getting it wrong could be lethal, both spiritually and physically, for those who receive these false words and an exponentially harsher judgment to those who have delivered these false words.

Here's one possible scenario: It becomes apparent that we've entered the 70th Week of Daniel, or obvious that we've entered the Great Tribulation/The Time of Jacob's Trouble. The rapture hasn't taken place. Israel has been militarily defeated and survivors have been forced into exile once again for fear of their lives. So, it comes down to this. Many believers will be compelled to ask, "Where is the promise of His coming?" After all, they've been taught as a fundamental tenet of the faith that an imminent rapture is the "blessed hope."

And, here is the "double whammy." "If we were wrong about the pre-tribulation rapture and we were wrong about the Final Return, what else have we been wrong about?" It will create the "perfect storm," for the "falling away" of many, as Paul wrote about in II Thes. 2:3. I Timothy 4:1, specifically, spells out that this "falling away" or "apostasy," depending upon your translation, is in the context of the last days.

I want you to notice something here. There's a reason why the doctrine of Dispensationalism and the Pre-Tribulation Rapture are joined at the hip. You know why that is? They complement each other by creating a separation between Israel and the Church. How convenient. How unscriptural. How dangerous. That false premise creates a doctrinal domino effect that, not only leads to error, but as previously stated, shipwreck. What this mentality is also saying is, Jacob's Trouble is Jacob's Problem.

It almost approaches the Early Church heresy of Marcionism. You know what Marcionism taught? Simply put, it taught that there was a god of the Old Testament and another God of the New Testament. The god of the Old Testament was something of a lesser and separate god whose main characteristic was wrath, while the god of the New Testament's main characteristic was love and forgiveness.

The belief in an Imminent Pre-Tribulation Rapture and/or the belief that the modern-day State of Israel represents the prophetic fulfillment of the Final Return, and, therefore, is invincible militarily, never to experience a successful invasion and dispersion from the Land, ever again, has this one common denominator: PRESUMPTION, which has historically always proven to be dangerous, even to the point of being spiritually and physically lethal.

Corrie Ten-Boom wrote this in a letter back in 1974, "In China, the Christians were told, "Don't worry, before the *tribulation comes you will be translated—raptured." Then came a terrible persecution. Millions of Christians were tortured to death. Later I heard a Bishop from China say, sadly, "We have failed. We should have made the people strong for persecution, rather than telling them Jesus would come first. Tell the people how to be strong in times of persecution, how to stand when the tribulation comes, to stand and not faint."*

Just to add a postscript to what Corrie Ten-Boom wrote, when China became a communist nation under Mao Tse Tung in 1949, many of the pastors who had been teaching this pre-tribulation rapture doctrine often found themselves in the same prison cells as those whom they had taught. And so, it was not unusual for these pastors to be spat upon by their former members as they passed by them, along with the rebuke: "you lied to us! You said we'd be raptured before anything like this happened!"

So, I've said all that to say this: teaching people to believe in the absolute certainty of an imminent pre-tribulation rapture and that modern-day Israel is confirmation of the Final Return of the Jewish People back to the Land, and that ALL Jews, wholesale, should be making aliyah ASAP under the premise that Israel will provide the only safe haven for the Jew from future persecution, is, I believe, irresponsible and ministerial malpractice at its worst.

All the malpractice insurance in the world won't be able to compensate for all the blood that's going to be on many teachers' hands, and I don't mean just physically. What are these teachers going to say, when it becomes crystal clear that they were wrong and that their end-time teachings and timelines had, literally, passed them by?

II Corinthians 7:10–"For the sorrow that is according to the will of God produces a repentance without regret, leading to salvation, but the sorrow of the world produces death."

And, this is perhaps, the most critical and most neglected consideration when discussing the reestablishment of the nation of Israel in 1948 and the question of the Final Return, although, for the vast majority of evangelical supporters of Israel, raising such a question at all is absurd, if not approaching the threshold of heresy and anti-semitism.

I would suggest to you that, generally speaking, what came of the Holocaust, was not a godly sorrow according to the will of God which produced a repentance leading to salvation, but rather, a worldly sorrow, the sorrow of a victim, which resulted in the defiant declaration of "Never Again!"

Adding to the recent tragedy was that of giving the wrong response. I would suggest to you that what came out of the horrific nightmare of the Holocaust, for the most part, was a people who were broke, but not broken and contrite in spirit.

I believe it would have been pleasing to God after those who had survived such an unimaginable and horrific event, and on the verge of the re-establishment of the nation of Israel, had offered up a corporate prayer to God, echoing that of II Chronicles 7:14, which in its intended context, was a word specifically given to Israel. "That if My *people who are called by My name humble themselves and pray and seek My face and turn from their wicked ways, then I will hear from heaven, will forgive their sin and will heal their land."*

God will certainly fulfill His covenant promises to Israel, including permanent possession of the Land, but as the case with the Children of Israel during the exodus, they could choose do it the easy way or the hard way. Because of their disobedience, what should have taken a few weeks to enter the Promised Land, took 40 years, and an entire generation, tainted by their past history of rebellion was disqualified from entering the Promised Land, perishing in the wilderness, whereby, a new generation would be permitted to enter in.

What I would submit to you is that what should and could have taken place immediately following the Holocaust was a recognition of God's judgment upon the Jewish People due to their generational predominant rebellion in refusing to acknowledge their sinful condition and recognize "their day of visitation" by the promised Messiah. There was a "worldly sorrow," but not the "godly sorrow" required of God "leading to repentance and salvation." Instead, they placed their trust in their own flesh, which declared, "Never Again!"

What should have led to repentance, resulting in their redemption, albeit a remnant, due to their continued disobedience and "trust in their own flesh" must now, by God's faithfulness to His Covenant, bring them to the place of devastation of a universal kind, having chosen an even harder path to their inheritance with respect to the

Land and fulfillment of their original calling, "to be a light to the nations."

And so, it should beg the question: Is present-day Israel the fulfillment of God's promised "Final Return" or for judgment as a prelude to their "Final Return" based upon God's criteria for entering the Land and possessing it, forever, as revealed in Scripture?

I believe the answer and overall message is essentially two-fold concerning the modern-day nation of Israel and why it is so critical to the Church's understanding and end-time ministry to the Jew in the "last days." One aspect of the message deals with, what I call, "The When (or IF) and Then Principle."

The other aspect is the hard word that the modern-day re-gathering of Israel of 1948 is not the "Final Return" as so many evangelicals ("friends" of Israel) interpret it, but God's re-gathering of Israel for judgment (chastisement), being set up for the "Time of Jacob's Trouble."

But, the end of the process will result in the remnant of Israel who does, in fact, return to take possession of the Land, forever—but, not until God has dealt with her, bringing her to that place of brokenness and repentance, who "look upon Him whom they have pierced," and finally meeting the God-given qualifications for entering into her permanent and eternally secure possession of the Land.

For the Jews, the Lord's Second Coming (Day of the Lord) and the Restoration of Israel was always considered a simultaneous and inextricably linked fulfillment resulting in the consummation of the age; that of Israel's consolation, comfort and restoration.

We refer to geographical Israel as the Holy Land. Is it called to be a Holy Land? Yes! In reality, is it a Holy Land? No! Why? Because a holy God requires a holy land to be inhabited by a holy people in which to dwell. Just as the high priest couldn't even enter the Holy of Holies in the Tabernacle or Temple of God unless he had first sanctified himself by taking off his normal priestly garments, wash, and then put on the special garments which were prescribed for the sacrifices which took him into the Holy of Holies.

He couldn't just enter the Tabernacle or Temple on his own terms, but only strictly according to God's terms. And, even if he was permitted to enter, he wasn't "home free." He had to conduct himself in a manner worthy of the owner of the dwelling and according to the strictest of instructions. If not, he didn't last long.

There is only one mentality that a true lover of Israel and the Jew can possess that will be representative of God's Heart and that which will be required, when it is no longer in vogue to take such a position—a position that is diminishing with each passing day. It won't be long when it will be at the risk of one's life to befriend a Jew.

It will be under such circumstances that, whatever was rooted in natural fascination and sentimentality, will be exposed, with only the genuine remaining. I believe it will be but a remnant proportional to that redeemed "remnant of Israel."

If you intend to be among the genuine "lovers of Israel" you'd better settle it right now, before the storm. Here's your biblical requirement and standard laid out as no other in the whole of Scripture. 2500 years ago, a Moabitess named Ruth made this remarkable statement to a Jewess named Naomi, a statement which the Jew will need to hear and see demonstrated by the Church in that day when the Jew will need her the most.

There are some who teach, even to the point of being giddy, that Jesus will be hosting a "marriage supper" on the heels of a pre-tribulation rapture," lasting the full seven years of the Seventieth Week of Daniel. That would mean that there would be great feasting and rejoicing in heaven right on through to the end of the "Time of Jacob's Trouble." Just ponder that for a moment.

There is a strange, and I will even go so far as to say, a perverse disconnect when believers can read Scriptures like Romans 9, 10 and 11 and can come up with the "blessed hope" as being that of an imminent rapture of the Church, with no thought of having any responsibility in Israel's redemption, or as one man has expressed it, a mentality that says, "Jacob's Trouble" is "Jacob's Problem."

There is a serious disconnect here, and worse, your testimony to the Jew just got tossed into the refuse heap!" And, what a perverse disconnect from the reality of what the vast majority of the Church is subjected to on a daily basis throughout much of the world. We should be embarrassed!

As to Replacement Theology, it denies continuity with Israel in one way and Dispensationalism denies it in another. Replacement theology makes the Church the new Israel, as it denies literal fulfillment to the many scriptures that promise the reconstitution of Israel as a distinctly Jewish nation. The Church's misplacement and spiritualization of the millennium, is in keeping with its historic disregard of the Jew, since the millennium exists for the sake of the further fulfillment of the still remaining covenant promises to Israel.

For this very purpose, Jewish identity has been miraculously preserved. The Early Church did not see the present age as the last, but understood itself as the first fruits of a larger eschatological harvest. The restoration of the kingdom to Israel was never a question of whether but when.

Acts 1:6 - "So when they had come together, they were asking Him, saying, "Lord, is it at this time You are restoring the kingdom to Israel?"

Act 3:18-21 - "But the things which God announced beforehand by the mouth of all the prophets, that His Christ would suffer, He has thus fulfilled. Therefore repent and return, so that your sins may be wiped away, in order that times of refreshing may come from the presence of the Lord; and that He may send Jesus, the Christ appointed for you, whom heaven must receive until the period of restoration of all things about which God spoke by the mouth of His holy prophets from ancient time."

Romans 11:25-29 - "For I do not want you, brethren, to be uninformed of this mystery—so that you will not be wise in your own estimation—that a partial hardening has happened to Israel until the fullness of the Gentiles has come in; and so all Israel will be saved; just as it is written, "The Deliverer will come from Zion, He will remove ungodliness from Jacob. This is My covenant with them, when I take away their sins. From the standpoint of the gospel they are enemies for your sake, but from the standpoint of God's choice they are beloved for the sake of the fathers; for the gifts and the calling of God are irrevocable."

Our view of Israel and the Church will be greatly determined by how we interpret the mystery. Does the mystery not revealed in other ages mean that the covenant with Israel has been completely fulfilled with the church, as the "new Israel" of the Spirit, replacing forever the historical nation? Or does the mystery reveal the church as a separate people of God with its own promises and destiny, as in Dispensational thought?

Replacement theology denies continuity with Israel in one way and Dispensationalism denies it in another. Replacement theology makes the church the new Israel, as it denies literal fulfillment to the many scriptures that promise the reconstitution of Israel as a distinctly Jewish nation. Dispensationalism, on the other hand, denies continuity with Israel based on its view that the church is a heavenly people, separate in calling and destiny from Israel. This strict dichotomy between the church and Israel is the basis for Dispensationalism's doctrine of a pre-tribulational rapture.

In the Dispensational view, the Church is looking for an any moment return of Christ that is not signaled by any preceding events of prophecy. In contrast, Israel's hope *awaits the return of Christ after the tribulation. This is the basis for Dispensationalism's theory of two peoples of God.*

The promise that the nations would partake in Israel's blessings was never imagined to cancel or reinterpret the great number of highly descriptive and detailed national promises that were never transferred to the church as the so-called, "new Israel" of replacement theology. That is the really misguided reckoning of a church that has historically boasted itself against the branches to its own incalculable loss.

As Paul warned, ignorance of "this mystery" exposes the Church to the pride of presumption, as it robs the Church of comprehending the true nature of the grace by which it stands. But what is worse, it robs God of our fuller appreciation of such an overwhelming display of Divine glory, and of its unspeakable cost. We have only to see Paul's enraptured response found in Romans 11:25-36 to such a sweeping vision of glory to imagine what ignorance of this mystery has cost the church throughout the centuries.

Worst of all, is Dual Covenant Theology. Why? Because, it directly skews the most critical aspect of faith---salvation, itself! Therefore, I have no reservation in categorizing this doctrine under a term that I tend to use sparingly— heresy!

So, what is Dual Covenant Theology? Simply put, it holds to the belief that the Old Covenant or the Law of Moses remains valid for Jews while the New Covenant only applies to non-Jews or Gentiles. It teaches that Jews can be saved without believing in the Messiah Jesus. God supposedly has a separate plan for the Jews and thus faith in the Messiah is not necessary.

For me, from the standpoint of interpretation, coming up with such an unscriptural and heretical view is not so much the result of twisting the Scriptures as it is in ignoring countless texts contrary to such a doctrine. In fact, it is a false gospel that strikes at the very heart of the true one! I will even take it one step farther and refer to those who promulgate in such teaching as "enemies of the cross of Christ." As Jesus warned, "Woe to the world because of it stumbling blocks! For it is inevitable that stumbling blocks come; but woe to that man through whom the stumbling block comes!" Matthew 18:6 - "but whoever causes one of these little ones who believe in Me to stumble, it would be better for him to have a heavy millstone hung around his neck, and to be drowned in the depth of the sea." Out of the entire Bible, next to the acceptance or rejection of Jesus as Lord and Savior, neglecting to take this verse to heart may be the most dangerous of all.

Chapter 5

REALIZATION: THE WHERE

"These shall escape from his hand: Edom, Moab, and the prominent people of Ammon"

The "Mountains" that Jesus says to "flee to" are by necessity outside of Judea/Israel proper but near enough to arrive at by foot or car. We know they are outside because He says "those who are there must flee" - He did not say "go to a different part of Judea," He's saying GET OUT OF DODGE. That urgency is also why they must be near enough to escape to by foot or by car. Catching a last minute flight out of Tel Aviv is not going to be an option; that notion will be more fully dispelled in chapter 8. Now, it just so happens that there is a mountain range very near to Judea but outside the borders of Israel. These mountains that Jesus says to flee to are very likely the contiguous mountain range in western Jordan and northeast Saudi Arabia, spanning from Amman to a new pseudo-state called NEOM (home of Mt. Sinai). So if understood either literally as mountainous areas or symbolic of the surrounding gentile nations, this geographic location of Jordan/Arabia fits perfectly with what Jesus is saying. In fact, when we examine the issue, there are simply no other available candidates.

FILLING MORE THAN ONE PURPOSE

Isn't it just like God to accomplish multiple things with one event? What if He could save a remnant of Jews AND frustrate the Antichrist at the same time? I believe that is precisely what the mountains of Jordan and Arabia will provide. Daniel 11 tells us specifically that the Antichrist will not be able to invade or subdue three distinct locations: Edom, Moab, and the "prominent people" or "best part" of Ammon. Ammon (now spelled Amman) is the capital city of Jordan today and lies in the heart of the country, at the north end of the Dead Sea. Just to the south of the city is Mt. Nebo, where Moses died, and that peak is the de facto beginning of the Jordanian mountains. They extend southward, through the lands the Bible calls Moab and Edom, into modern day Saudi Arabia. And they just so happen to run into Mt Sinai (called Jebel al Lawz by the Arabs). Are we to believe this mountainous geography bordering Israel that Daniel mentions as a place of escape from the Antichrist has nothing to do with the "Mountains" that Jesus tells the Jews to flee towards?

Let's reiterate: Moses received the Law on Mt. Sinai in Arabia. He died on Mt. Nebo in Moab in central Jordan. Those two mountains of the Exodus could well be the beginning and end of the final journey of Israel during their Time of Trouble. Note that both Elijah the prophet and the Apostle Paul followed this <u>same route</u> to seek God when they came to the end of themselves. They intentionally went back to "where it all began" for their people. When Jerusalem is surrounded by the armies of the Antichrist half way through the final seven years, we know the Abomination of Desolation is next. This "next door" region is not only where so much Biblical history has taken place, but it is where the Church should be preparing to receive the untold thousands who will escape. The Word of God is true and alive. Bible Prophecy is real and will be played out in the dust of Arab lands. Where else could these "mountains" be?

When Jesus says "when you see these things flee to the mountains," that doesn't mean that when armies surround Jerusalem, that everybody in North Carolina must flee to the Smokies, or if you're in Missouri, go head for the Ozarks...
- Joel Richardson

EYES TO SEE

Words are great but there is no substitute for visual aids! Study the maps on the following 4 pages and try to visualize this highway that those who listen to God and flee Israel will be using. A note on the land of Edom: the borders of that kingdom increased greatly between the time of the Exodus and the Babylonian captivity so that it completely engulfed the lands of Midian. So the Edom in the end times is likely far larger than we think.

MAP #1
The "Mountains" on the escape route out of "Judea"

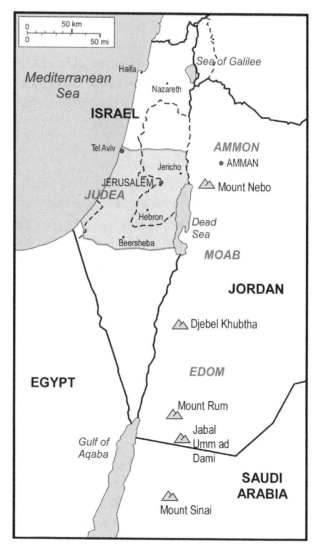

Image by Mark Davidson, 2019

MAP #2
Locations of Ammon, Moab, and Edom at the time of the Exodus

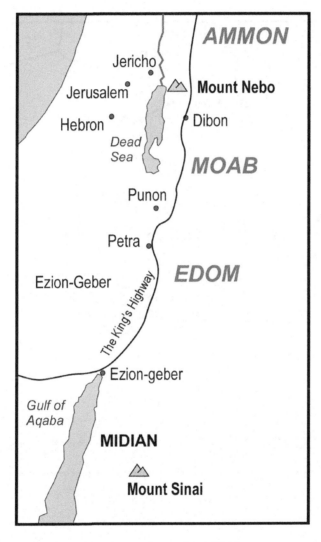

Image by Mark Davidson, 2019

MAP #3
Territory of Edom in Jeremiah 49 and Ezekiel 25.
"From Teman to Dedan"

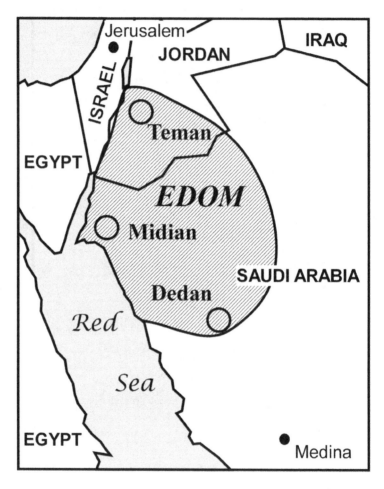

Image by Mark Davidson, 2019

MAP #4
New mega-city/pseudo-state NEOM to be created in overlapping Biblical territories Edom, Midian and Arabia and containing Mt. Sinai

Image by Mark Davidson, 2019

Chapter 6

REALIZATION: THE WHY (BACK TO SINAI)

"I did not go up to Jerusalem, instead I went to Arabia"

As mentioned in the last chapter, the "why" of this great drama has a lot to do with going back to where it all began for the Jewish people so they can come back to their God. The promise to Abraham, Isaac and Jacob was for a specific land, that land we call Israel. At various times throughout history, God has allowed the Jews to be evicted from that land for their disobedience. This final dispersion, while it will hurt far worse than any time before it, is ultimately for their good. As pointed out in Revelation 12, God will reveal this to them as He speaks to the Woman in that wilderness during those final years of Trouble. As Hosea 2 says, "I will allure her, bring her into the wilderness and speak tenderly to her there, and will make the Valley of Achor a door of hope." Achor means "trouble" and that location was established as a burial ground with a proclamation by a man named Yeshua: "The LORD will trouble you this day." Through that very real "door of trouble," Jesus will offer Israel hope. In that light, is it any wonder Paul puts it this way in Colossians 4,

"Pray that God would open to us a door for the word, to speak the mystery of Christ." From the Valley of Achor north of the Dead Sea, across into Ammon and Moab where Moses died, then the journey turns south.

SINAI IN ARABIA

In his letter to the Galatians, Paul twice mentions Mt. Sinai being located in Arabia. By definition, Arabia cannot be within the borders of Israel or Egypt, it must be in Saudi Arabia. It is outside the scope of this book to defend that particular point–see Joel Richardson's new book "Mount Sinai in Arabia" and the new website by The Clarion Project's Ryan Mauro at SinaiInArabia.com–but it has always been clear to me that even a cursory understanding of the geographic journey in Exodus requires Horeb/Sinai to be in the land of ancient Midian: modern day Saudi Arabia. Look at what Paul does after he is saved by the risen Jesus on the road to Damascus: "But when it pleased God…to reveal His Son in me…I did not immediately confer with flesh and blood, nor did I go up to Jerusalem to those who were apostles before me; but I went to Arabia…Then after three years I went up to Jerusalem." I do not believe those details are just for Paul's journey, as with all Scripture they are for our benefit, we upon whom the end of the age has nearly come.

This means that Elijah also took this journey as he had to "flee Judea" into Arabia though the southern Jordanian mountains from Jezebel (1 Kings 19). Even the greatest prophet in Israel's history "had enough" and reached the end of himself and God drove him–after feeding him–to Sinai.

So we have examples in both Old and New Testaments of two of the most powerful Jews to ever live going through the Jordanian mountains into Arabia to seek God where it all began. In God's providence, though widely known to ancient Israel, it seems He has deliberately kept the true location of Sinai "under wraps" to the vast majority of the world (and the Jews, and the Church) for thousands of years. But that lid is about to be blown off by Saudi Arabia.

NEOM

So what about this "NEOM" place we have been referencing? Take a look at Map #4 in Chapter 5 to see exactly where it is and what is contained within. What is the plan for it exactly? In October 2017, Saudi Crown Prince Mohammad bin Salman accounted the launch of "NEOM." In his words, "NEOM is born from the ambition of Saudi Arabia's Vision 2030 to see the country develop into a pioneering and thriving model of excellence in various and important areas of life. NEOM aims to thrive the transformation of the Kingdom into a leading global hub through the introduction of value chains of industry and technology…NEOM is developed to be independent of the Kingdom's existing governmental framework, excluding sovereignty…NEOM is situated on one of the world's most prominent economic arteries, through which nearly a tenth of the world's trade flows. Its strategic location will also facilitate the zone's rapid emergence as a global hub that connects Asia, Europe and Africa, enabling 70% of the world's population to reach it in under eight hours… The site will also become the main entrance to the King

Salman Bridge, linking Asia and Africa, which will add to the zone's economic significance. NEOM's land mass will extend across the Egyptian and Jordanian borders, rendering NEOM the first private zone to span three countries" (press release from NEOM.com).

Read all about it at NEOM.com, but pay special attention to the "King Salman Bridge" aspect, especially the fact that it links Egyptian desert to the Jordanian mountains. Friends, *this is the exact route of the Exodus the children of Israel took.* I'll bet you dollars to doughnuts that the Bridge will even be built on the exact location of the Red Sea crossing (connecting to Nuweiba Beach in Egypt - see the compelling evidence from Ryan Mauro at https://jabalmaqla.com/israelites-red-sea-crossing-location/). The one thing the Saudis aren't yet saying publicly is what they DO acknowledge privately, that Mt. Sinai is there in NEOM. It will be preserved as a worldwide pilgrimage site and tourist attraction. Both Ryan Mauro and Joel Richardson have been producing stunning evidence of not just the fire-scarred Sinai itself but all of the geologic features from the Biblical Exodus account in this region now dubbed NEOM. God is very clearly up to something. And as usual, He will accomplish more than one objective at the same time.

For a very recent update on NEOM and how they are expecting new international residents and businesses very soon, see this article from Bloomberg Jan, 16, 2019:

Saudi Arabia said it will start building the first residential area in a proposed $500 billion futuristic city that's become a symbol of Crown Prince Mohammed bin Salman's ambitions for life after oil. *The kingdom plans to start work on Neom Bay in the first quarter this year, according to the state-run Saudi Press Agency. The area will have "white beaches, a mild climate and an attractive investment environment," SPA said. Phase one will be completed by 2020, according to the agency. The planned megacity, unveiled more than a year ago, is part of the prince's grand plan to bolster non-oil revenue and attract foreign investment with eye-popping proposals to transform the economy, including two other tourism developments. Neom is to be financed by the Saudi government, its sovereign wealth fund, and local and international investors. The project includes a bridge spanning the Red Sea, connecting the proposed city to Africa. Some 10,000 square miles (25,900 square kilometers) have been allocated for the development of the urban area, which will stretch into Jordan and Egypt. Prince Mohammed, in an interview with Bloomberg in October, referred to the first phase of the project as the Neom Riviera. "Neom city will be completed in 2025," he said, adding without elaborating that "there are interesting partners in the Middle East and globally. Interesting names." A number of facilities will be opened at Neom by the end of this year, SPA reported, without providing further details. The private airport at the site will be used for commercial flights by year-end, it said.*

What is NEOM? It is mostly autonomous ultra hi-tech futuristic giant city-state linking the mountains of Jordan to Mt. Sinai and Egypt, with Israel in the center of it all. The Gospel now has an open door, public churches may even be built. Could this be not only the destination for the Jews seeking God in their darkest hours, but the "headquarters" for those "preparing the way"? I urge you to think and pray on that.

THE WILDERNESS JOURNEY

My interview with Joel Richardson continued on this very topic and he offered a stunning glimpse into the Biblical "wilderness" that Israel has never really left behind.

In Hosea it says that in the last days the Lord will allure Israel into the wilderness. This is not just any vague general wilderness. It's the wilderness of the exodus. It actually says right in Hosea. It says that it's the place where she will rejoice as when she was young, ie., when she was a newlywed, when she was zealous in her commitment to Me.

The idea is that the Lord is going to bring Israel back into the wilderness of the exodus. There's no question that the concept of the second exodus is the very clearly taught theme throughout the Bible, throughout Isaiah in particular and Jeremiah. The culmination of the Lord's entire plan of redemption will take place there in the wilderness from Sinai all the way up through Edom and Moab, then all the way up to the desert outside of Judea. So if you're to follow the exodus path out of Saudi Arabia, up through Jordan, and then around the top of the Dead Sea, past Jericho, toward Jerusalem, that is the biblical wilderness. That is the concept of the wilderness that was deeply embedded into Israel's mind.

When you go there to the land, you see it. When John the Baptist went out into the wilderness, again, it was not just a vague wilderness, it was the beginning of the exodus wilderness near Jericho. When you go into the Judean wilderness, you're stepping back onto the path from which they entered the land; you're reversing the exodus. John the Baptist was going back out into the wilderness. The wilderness is the place where you learn how to depend on God. You're no longer depending on the luxuries of modern appliances, and civilization, and comforts. From a biblical mindset, the desert has always been the place from where you are forced to rely on God and that's where He provides for you. Just like Israel did in the exodus when the Lord provided water from the rock, Manna from heaven, quail, etc. He provided for them, he protected them, and he tenderly cared for them.

There have been a handful of Christian writers that have written about Israel fleeing specifically to Petra or to Edom. But because I believe that Mount Sinai is in Saudi Arabia, I believe Israel will flee into the desert, all the way down to Sinai in northwest Saudi Arabia.

PREPARE THE HIGHWAY OF THE LORD

What if we just took the words of Isaiah the Prophet literally?

> The voice of one crying in the wilderness: Prepare the way of the LORD; <u>make straight in the desert a highway for our God</u> (Isaiah 40).

> Go out through the gates! <u>Prepare the highway for my people to return</u>! Smooth out the road; pull out the boulders; raise a flag for all the nations to see" (Isaiah 62).

To be sure, John the Baptist took it literally and lived across the Jordan to the north of the Dead Sea in the desert/wilderness of Moab. As we know, Jesus identified him with the Elijah who was to come. But He also said Elijah is coming again, before the Day of the Lord/Return of Jesus Christ. That gives a profound end-time meaning to Isaiah and the task at hand. Malachi the Prophet mentions Mt. Sinai as part of the equation in Malachi 4:4-5:

> *Remember the Law of Moses, My servant, which I commanded him in Horeb for all Israel,*
> *with the statutes and judgments. Behold, I will send you Elijah the prophet before the coming of the great and dreadful day of the LORD.*

As we have seen over and over, when Israel flees to the mountains, they will be taking a prescribed path from the area of Mt. Nebo in Jordan to Mt. Sinai in Arabia. This path will have to be "paved" beforehand to some degree. A road that can accommodate thousands of people is called a highway. Does this mean we need to build a new one? Or clear off an old one that already exists? The "King's Highway" (see Map #2 in Chapter 5) is an ancient roadway stretching from Egypt through Edom and Moab and Ammon to Assyria (northern Iraq). It is first mentioned in Numbers 20 when Israel could not pass though Edom's land– this time, they will. It will get them all the way to NEOM as a matter of fact.

In the critical prophecy of Isaiah 19, it starts off telling us of the "Kingdom against Kingdom" wars Jesus told us as a sign to watch for between the "Kingdom of the South."

Egypt and the "Kingdom of the North" will be led by the fierce Assyrian, the Antichrist. This is during the first 3.5 years of the final seven, during which time the "highway" next door must be cleared/established/protected. But it ends in a glorious promise when the Prince of Peace returns:

> *In that day there will be a highway from Egypt to Assyria, and the Assyrian will come into Egypt and the Egyptian into Assyria, and the Egyptians will serve with the Assyrians. In that day Israel will be one of three with Egypt and Assyria—a blessing in the midst of the land, whom the LORD of hosts shall bless, saying, Blessed is Egypt My people, and Assyria the work of My hands, and Israel My inheritance (Isaiah 19:23-24).*

Christian, <u>you</u> can be a part of this preparation.

WHAT HAS BEEN DONE? WHAT IS BEING DONE NOW?

Due to major misunderstanding, misapplication and mistrust among Christians, this work, if it has begun at all, is barely in the infant stages. The following three Chapters detail these issues. But I truly believe our Father is gathering the workers for this great task right now as you read this.

PART 3: WHAT WE MUST UN-DO

Chapter 7

MISUNDERSTANDING: GOD WILL DO THIS WITHOUT THE CHURCH

"Great fear came upon all the church and upon all who heard these things"

The most common objection you will hear from other Christians is, basically, "God will do this without us." That He will tell them directly to flee to the mountains, He directly will feed them, He directly will protect them. It goes without saying that every Christian should readily agree that our great God can do whatever He wants, whenever He wants, however He wants. This is not in dispute in any way - this book would dare not challenge that assertion. We would say, in fact, the one and only thing He *cannot* do is lie. Numbers 23:19, Titus 1:2 and Hebrews 6:18 all testify to this. He will not, cannot, break His word. If He has spoken and proclaimed it in Scripture it *must* be done. If there is anything written that does not happen exactly as He said, not only is the character of God mutilated, but *Satan wins the entire war.* That is what the temptation of Jesus in the wilderness was all about after all, getting God's word to fail. And that's the point, God has spoken on this.

WITH CHRIST IN US, WE CAN DO ALL THINGS

Putting aside the theological gymnastics necessary to believe God will speak directly to hundreds of thousands (or millions) of unbelieving Jews all at once, and for them to know Who exactly is speaking, where exactly will they be sent? Empty caves? What will be waiting for them when they arrive? Barren nothingness? As the Scriptures we have reviewed tell us, a time of preparation will precede their arrival. A preparation by a people —which will probably be a predominately Gentile group of Christians—is required. And yes, it must be done in the place and in the way that He has already spoken it. Are we as the Church ready to commit to such a preparatory work, even if we don't believe we will be around to see it utilized?

I appeal now to those who haven't been fully tracking with this book. Those who maybe think the Church will be removed from the earth prior to the command given to flee. Let's say that's right, that the Church will either be removed completely or have literally no role in telling the Jews when to go, and where to go and feed them once they arrive. I suggest that, even if this notion is correct, the Church *still* needs to do this work. And we need to start doing it now. We must take this opportunity we have as lights of the world to think, to plan, to plow, to organize habitations and travel routes, to set aside physical and spiritual food in those places, so that when the time comes, provision will be there. In the next chapter we will examine why those who have had this inclination almost always made a huge error in planning—they have the *wrong location*. Can we agree that no matter what your current view of the Church's role in Jacob's Trouble will be, the Church can have a role beforehand? And since we don't know at this point how much longer we have, it would be very prudent to begin this work now?

I ask you to ponder this: is it compatible with the New Testament to say that the Church is not responsible to do this work? The Ministry of the Holy Spirit *is* to reveal the Will of the Father to us, the Church. Things that were, that are, and things yet to come (John 14:26, 16:13). The Ministry of the Spirit though us is glorious! Since we ourselves are an epistle of Christ, written not with ink but by the Spirit of the living God; we have such hope, we use great boldness of speech (2 Corinthians 3). It is *through the Church* that God's plans are made manifest on the earth (Ephesians 3) - what other way is even hinted at in the Bible?

Are Christians just *afraid* of fulfilling the calling to minister to Israel in their greatest time of Trouble? We would rather run and hide - in heaven or in our comfy bunkers - than deliver that final martyr witness? This is a huge problem because it is precisely the *opposite* of what Revelation 12:11 says we should be doing. It seems to me that history is repeating itself. Just like in Acts 5 when some Christians tried to withhold and con the Church and therefore the Holy Spirit; the consequences were severe—and "great fear came on all the Church."

WHAT ABOUT THE MANNA, QUAIL AND RAVENS?

Many times Christians will mention God's supernatural provision for Israel with manna and quail and how He chose ravens to function as a "wait staff" to feed Elijah in the wilderness. They will use this instance of God's provision as "proof" that God will not need the faithful service of the Church during the time when Israel will flee. As mentioned above, there is no reason to deny God *can* provide without any assistance from His servants, but we see the principle demonstrated continuously throughout Scripture that He delights in using His people to accomplish His will. Yes, the provision to Israel during the Exodus and to Elijah during the 3.5 year famine was supernatural, but is this a valid precedent looking forward to Jacob's Trouble? I say no.

First thing is the means of provision. The manna was direct from heaven, no doubt, but look at Jesus' words about it in John 6. The door now seems to be closed on that means of provision being repeated. Yeshua is the "bread that came from heaven" and it is only partaking of Him that will save Israel. Now to the quail and ravens. It may have been supernatural in that humans were not involved, but those animals were not supernatural beings. They were utilized by God to perform a function that was needed to keep His promises. These are also not good comparisons looking forward for different reasons. In the case of the nation in the wilderness fed by the quail, it was given to those in belief/faith. It's debatable whether God would have ever provided the quail at all if the people hadn't complained about the manna not being good enough. It was only through God's friendship with Moses that many of these things were even accomplished. Remember that Israel had just been brought out of Egypt with multiple, dramatic and powerful supernatural signs they could *see*. They continually saw the Lord prove Himself to them in the smoke and fire day after day, night after night. They corporately knew their God and knew He was right there with them (not just some individuals, all of them). This is a completely different scenario than the end time Israel will face. The Jews who will flee Judea to the mountains will be in corporate *unbelief*. They will not know who Yeshua is and have not relied on Him, but rather upon their own strength. The mindset of "never again" is a big reason why they will be in that predicament at all. In the case of Elijah being fed by the ravens, they were given to an individual man of God. That one man—a prophet at that—who was on mission with acts yet to perform. The parallels for end time Israel just aren't there.

Secondly, there was no other set of "God's people" for Him to utilize. In the Exodus, any people they did run into were not hospitable to say the least (Edomites, Moabites, Midianites). In Elijah's case, he was intentionally on the run and was taking a path devoid of other people. The polar opposite is the case with the flight of Israel at the end of the age. They will seek and find others to feed them and explain to them exactly what is happening. Remember, those who are fleeing from the Antichrist will have been warned beforehand by the Church of the exact steps to take. God has a people this time and He will take great joy in using them. So once again, our Lord is obviously capable of anything, but this type of thing is not what He has ordained as provision for the refugees from Jerusalem during the time of Jacob's Trouble.

For every "What about the manna and the ravens?" I ask, "What about Esther and Joseph?" These were examples of people used by God to deliver Israel wholesale. As Fred London stated in Chapter 4, these are the correct archetypes for the Church in the last seven years. God clearly used those willing all-too-human vessels to save the nation from annihilation - this is the template, not doing it without us. Do you think Joseph felt like a hero in that hole his brothers threw him into or in that prison cell accused of rape? Esther was all alone in her resistance before the most powerful man in the world; I bet she was never planning on leaving that throne room alive. Friends, that is exactly the situation Jesus is looking to work "great exploits" through. It's really as simple as this: do you know your God and does He know you? Think of it this way: Jesus could have just removed Paul's blindness and given him the Holy Spirit immediately right there on the road to Damascus. Instead, He preferred to let Paul stumble blind on the rest of the journey and then use the Church in the person of Ananias to heal and baptize him. In the final seven years of the age, blinded Jews will be leaving Israel again and the Church is still His instrument to deliver salvation, physical and eternal.

WHAT ABOUT MESSIANIC JEWS IN ISRAEL NOW?

So shouldn't this task of preparing for and accomplishing this great future task fall to the believing Jews in the land of Israel? Well, not unlike the Gentile Church, there is division on some issues, not the least of which is the belief in a future time of Jacob's Trouble. As we saw in Chapter 2, this is a major sticking point to many. But here is some great news: there are more Jewish believers in Jesus in the land of Israel now than at any time since the original Church! Not such great news is they still only number about 15,000-20,000 among a total Jewish population of over 6 million. The witness of the predominantly Gentile Church is needed today and also in the days ahead.

When in Israel in 2017, I met Pastor Israel Pochtar at his place of worship in Ashdod. He is a Jewish man who has been born again and is a fiery leader doing wonderful work all over the country. The Holy Spirit connection was very strong and another Pastor friend I was traveling with suddenly realized he had already met Mr. Pochtar several years before. God was at work! I have kept in communication with Pastor Pochtar ever since then and seek to partner with him however possible. The work they are doing is also now being attacked from all sides by great opposition—book of Acts stuff indeed. He graciously agreed to answer a few of my questions for this book.

I asked, "As a Jewish believer in Israel, has the openness to the Gospel increased recently? Has the opposition to it? Have both?"

Yes, we have seen a tremendous increase in openness and interest in the Gospel, especially among secular Israelis. Our humanitarian projects form the foundation of reaching Israelis from all strata of society, as we tend to their physical and spiritual needs. The more we expand our projects, the more Israelis we are able to reach with the Gospel. Interestingly enough, this trend has gone hand-in-hand with the persecutions that we've been experiencing. Praise God, we're seeing God using the strategies of the enemy against him, by using the publicity in the media to shine a light on the love and salvation message of Jesus.

I asked, "As a Pastor of a congregation so close to Gaza, do you feel more separated from Muslims or more compelled to share the Gospel with them?"

We definitely feel more compelled to share the Gospel with Muslims, since we understand that our battle is not against flesh and blood, but against spiritual powers which are deceiving mankind into following the schemes of the devil. We believe that God loves the Muslims and also wants to see them saved.

I asked, "Are the 144,000 of Revelation 7 and 14 all Messianic Jews like yourself?"

We aren't sure, but we're praying for revelation with regards to this. We do understand that God's plan of Israel's restoration relies heavily on the Messianic Jews in the land, and that we are here at this time for a very specific purpose, along with the Gentile believers who have joined hands with us.

I asked, "How do you see your personal role during the time of Jacob's Trouble?"

We believe that Jacob's trouble is a recurring theme found throughout the Bible and the history of modern man, as the spirit of anti-christ works through certain indi-

viduals and groups to target the Jewish people for annihilation and to feed antisemitism throughout the world. Our role as Jewish believers, along with gentile believers, are to wage war in the heavenlies and to tear down the strategies and the works of Satan against the church and the nation of Israel, and to help the Jewish people understand and answer the call of Jesus to walk in their calling as a priestly nation, sanctified unto the Lord.

I asked, "Are Christian churches in Israel of any type or denomination (Jewish, Arab etc) making any kind of practical preparation for the coming time of Jacob's Trouble? If so, what specifically is needed most from the Church in the rest of the world?"

Not that I know of, but it is definitely a good idea for the body of Messiah to be prepared, spiritually and physically, to weather any storms that might come, be it war, persecution, lack of finances and resources, isolation and division. Currently the body of believers in Israel do face financial struggles mostly with regards to rent, administration, humanitarian stock etc, and are believing God to open fountains of provision.

ONE THING THAT KEEPS COMING UP

Over and over the theme of not working together, not acting strategically for the days to come is expressed. This saddens and frustrates me. Even in the land of Israel, with so much in common, there is still that lack of vision for what is around the corner...how is this possible? We will address this more in Chapter 9, but not working together as one body cannot continue. Many of us are starting to awaken to the fact of the end time calling the Church has, and the call to unity must be sounded loud and clear from around the world, until it reaches Jerusalem itself. King Yeshua's own prayer in John 17 appeals for this.

This lack of vision and cooperation is not always intentional. In fact, I would not question the heart of any Gospel minister in Israel today, only the "intentionality" of common mission. Don't misunderstand: becoming and making disciples has not changed or taken a back seat to anything, nor should it. Just as in the New Testament, the reality of brotherhood is automatic upon salvation, but the act of brotherhood and the expression of Christlike love is a conscious choice and a daily decision. The thrust of holy mission in the love of the brethren to network together and make strategic preparations for those final seven years is a deliberate act, one I pray will be entered into by thousands more in the very near future.

SHIRKING OUR RESPONSIBILITY

Over the past several years, mulling these questions over in my mind and debating with fellow Christians as to our role in that final time of Jacob's Trouble, I can only come to one ultimate conclusion: one way or another, the Gentile Church is looking for ways to shirk our responsibility to the Jews. Yes, *responsibility*. Paul cuts to the root of this attitude in Romans 11:11-32 particularly in verse 18. The very idea that we can separate the destiny of the Gentile Church from physical Israel is absurd. Our destiny is shared. Salvation ("Yeshua") is of the Jews—He is today the Lion of Judah—and He is only coming again when the

Jews of Jerusalem call for Him. This is the reality of a continuum of time, not a finished historical event 2,000 years ago. Until "all Israel is saved" the creation will groan, and the Spirit within His Church will groan. No matter how many ways we deny it, the immutable truth remains that it is the Gentile Church's responsibility to minister to Israel, all the way until the bitter end. When God's "midnight call" goes out, Daniel's 70th Week will move inexorably towards the conclusion we all await, but will He find faithfulness in the Church?

We all should be familiar with "The Great Commission" in Matthew 28. As I touched on in Chapter 2, this certainly must apply to Christians of all time (this has been the accepted orthodox view for two millennia). Here is something that our Lord said there that we need to read over very carefully: "I am with you always, even to the end of the age." The NIV renders it "the *very* end of the age." Young's translation says "the *full* end of the age." Literally it says the *"entire completion."* Does this leave any room for the Church (be it Gentile or Jew) to be gone for even one millisecond? Didn't Jesus say as much when He told us the Gospel must be preached to all nations and then the end would come? No more Gospel preaching = Jesus on earth as King of the nations. There is no in between time period/dispensation even alluded to in the Scriptures, either Old or New Testaments. The bottom line is simply this: the Holy Spirit-filled Church *must must must* be here, and specifically in Israel to "prepare the way of the Lord." There is no leaving of this responsibility before Jesus returns to rule, unless we die first.

GOD HAS CHOSEN WHAT IS WEAK IN THE WORLD TO SHAME THE STRONG

There is nothing new under the sun. Just as Paul told us, "For you see your calling, brethren, that not many wise according to the flesh, not many mighty, not many noble, are called." We know we can't fulfill this great responsibility to Israel in the last 7 years of the age in ourselves. But we also know that whatever God proclaims, it will be done, as weak and ineffective as we are. He does this *on purpose* so that "no flesh can glory in His presence." *Jesus will be glorified in our frailty.* In the Gospels or in the book of Acts when the Disciples cast out demons or healed someone, who did that? God of course, but *through* the Church. That's the understanding we need to come to. We are His chosen method; to Israel and to the Nations who hate her.

To say "God will do this without the Church" is to *deny God's already settled plan.* I don't want to go there. You don't either. Let us resolve to agree with Him, whatever that may mean for our flesh. Yes, the Antichrist nations who surround Israel will soon unite as one and attack - empowered by Satan himself. They will seem very "strong" indeed. When the Saints are "overcome" by that Beast that means they are on the scene getting in his way, figuratively and literally. Those who "love not their lives even when faced with death" are exemplified throughout the final 3.5 years–that's the ultimate meaning and fulfillment of our calling as the Church of Jesus Christ. When the Lord tells the martyrs in heaven "just a little while longer until the rest are killed as you were," those are they who have taken their calling and responsibility to

Israel seriously, have counted the cost and are willing to pay the price. It is through *that* witness of the final Church martyrs that the "strong" enemies of God and His Messiah and His nation will be shamed and judged guilty. Our blood along with the blood of the Jews on their hands is what justifies the Wrath of God falling upon them. Let us glory in God alone as He does the impossible though us during those final years.

Chapter 8

MISAPPLICATION: FLEEING TO THE WEST

"For whom the LORD loves He corrects, Just as a father the son in whom he delights"

Art Katz was a giant of the Faith: a New York City Jew who grew into an ardent Atheist, but was pursued and found by the Lord Yeshua in his mid-30s. After his conversion he traveled and wrote and taught in public for over 40 years, always with the burden of Israel on his heart. To his great credit, he was an iconoclast who was unafraid not only in the midst of enemies but of Christian friends. Often speaking hard words to crowds of believers, his brokenness before the Lord was evident. In 2007 he went home to glory. One issue he revisited over and over was the coming time of Jacob's Trouble. It drove his ministry to the point of literally building a compound in Minnesota in anticipation of housing many Jews who would need a place to flee to if/when the Time of Trouble began. Needless to say, his heart cannot be questioned, and the impact of his message on the Body has been tangible. However, his geography was off target.

BUYING A PLANE TICKET WILL NOT BE AN OPTION

There are ministries today led by dear brothers and sisters who are teaching "preparation" for this eventuality: in the wrong place. First and foremost, our preparation has got to be spiritual so as to not deny Christ (see <u>Spiritual Prepper</u>). Second, it has to be Scriptural. If we have been led by Holy Spirit to provide a place for the Jews during Jacob's Trouble, we need to take special care to stick to what the Bible actually says. Not extrapolating meanings that are not clearly laid out. That doesn't mean extrapolation doesn't have its place—hidden gems for the wise man to mine is a real phenomenon (Proverbs 25:2)—but we cannot build doctrine on this technique. The "big things" on the prophetic calendar are clearly stated. What God wants done will not need to be extrapolated, it will just need to be obeyed.

As we have already seen in this book, the words of Jesus on this time of Jacob's Trouble are clear and simple and precise. The words of the Prophets on this are matter of fact. If anything has to be un-sealed or un-earthed it has been hidden in plain sight all along. Despite the power and influence of the United States, despite the millions of Jews currently in her and in Europe, the Bible says nothing about those nations harboring the Jews within them. It talks about the Jews specifically in and around Jerusalem in the nation of Israel going to local places to flee from the Antichrist. It does not specially teach that Jews in any other nation will even be persecuted. Now, we may reasonably assume this will be the case, but that's not the same as having it written on the page. That doesn't mean it is wrong or violating Scripture to do so, but it isn't what the Bible says either. Hiding Jews in America, Europe, the other countries of the West—or any other nation than what the Bible specifically lists—is not un-Biblical, but it is extra-Biblical.

There are some teachings that go even further and need to be debunked right now: the "wings of the great eagle" are not airplanes from the United States (or any other country). The "wilderness" is not the forests of North America. The entire Western culture is one of obsession with ourselves and our own nations. Nowhere is this more evident than the United States in the past 100 years. As the years go on, the more self-obsessed we become. It's all about us and our country, all the time, every day. Nowhere else in the world do other countries ask "where are we mentioned in Bible prophecy?" We must admit firstly that God is not in covenant with America, nor with any western nation, only with Israel. And since that everlasting covenant must be preserved, the people and land to which it applies is the "apple of God's eye." God doesn't hate America, He doesn't want to destroy America, but He didn't choose America to put His name in. The Jews won't be fleeing to America. The Jews of Israel will not be able to get on an airplane and escape to hide out in America or any Western nation. Like all other prophecies in the Bible, the context is *Middle Eastern*.

The bottom line is, there will not be time. When Jesus says, "Let him who is on the housetop not go down to take anything out of his house. And let him who is in the field not go back to get his clothes" He is stressing the absolute immediacy of the action. Go and run and don't look back. "Remember Lot's wife" indeed. When He says, "But woe to those who are pregnant and to those who are nursing babies in those days! And pray that your flight may not be in winter or on the Sabbath," He is stressing that travel on foot will be required. On the Sabbath, Israel is basically shut down. You can't even get a taxi. There is a 0.0% chance of anyone going to Ben Gurion to fly to JFK. As if that airspace will even be open to civilian traffic when the Assyrian invades?

GET READY TO LOSE COMFORT

Whether it is admitting that the mountains the Jews must flee to are in the Middle East, or that your nation in the West may be in the throes of upheaval, terrorism and war during this time, discomfort will set in. That really isn't anything new to the Christian walk, or it shouldn't be. It flies in the face of the Euro-American ethos, but to be "a nation at ease" is not a place were we want to be, Biblically speaking. Our God is "zealous for Jerusalem and for Zion with great zeal." This is an ongoing contention and the time of Jacob's Trouble is the culmination of that controversy. We Western Christians tend to view the Great Tribulation myopically as in "how will that affect me" when it should give us the wider view and lead us to pray "how can I be a part of what God will be doing". As I mentioned in Chapter 1, this story is not over, we are right in the middle of it. And if we know our God, it will change our thinking about the end times from "scary" to "thrilling."

This is the great danger of chasing after philosophies like "free speech," "democracy," "capitalism" and "patriotism" instead of the Gospel and the Kingdom of God. Satan loves it when we waste our time, and there is no lack of time wasting in modern society. Even in my lifetime (43 years as of this writing) the increase in time wasted by the average person has increased to the point of becoming an epidemic. *This author raises hand as guilty, by the way.* From endless hours of video games growing up to endless hours volunteering for political candidates, I know about non-Kingdom related time wasting. Now, my philosophy is this: Give me a sold-out, Spirit-filled Christian obsessed with the Kingdom who disdains politics over a political activist who goes to Church and gives lip service to Jesus—all day long.

Life in America and the West will become more and more uncomfortable as the reality of God's election of the Jew and the land of Israel comes into focus. I do not pretend to know the depths of the discomfort these nations of the West will experience, but full-scale invasion by enemy nations, nuclear war and societal collapse are not off the table. *If we view whatever happens in the light of correction from our Father, I believe we will shine in whatever nation we reside.* Just keep Zion in prayerful sight and be willing to say yes if He calls you to get to those very specific mountains; but Israel will not be fleeing here to the West.

Chapter 9

MISTRUST: NOT WORKING TOGETHER AS ONE BODY

"We should not trust in ourselves but in God who raises the dead"

The greatest source of sadness, discouragement and questioning of my faith the past several years has been from fellow Christian ministries, specifically those in the Middle East or those who concentrate there. Even after meeting face to face and exchanging jubilant exclamations of "oh yes let's work together," phone calls are not answered, emails are not returned, friend requests on social media are not accepted. The only reason I can discern for this is a simple lack of trust. If we cannot trust our own Brethren in Christ, whom can we trust? Many times I see as Paul does in Philippians 2:21 "all seek their own." Where are the Timothys who will work together and not pursue our own self-interests? Tact is understandable, even necessary. But secrecy among Christians called into the same arena is not.

PERSONAL EXAMPLES

Several years ago I began volunteering for a wonderful organization called Voice of the Martyrs. Being "voices" for our persecuted Brothers and Sisters around the world is a great and Godly work, and they hold regular conferences throughout America. When they are near me, I attend and have gotten to meet some absolute giants of the faith. When a connection is made with those with ministries/networks in Syria and Iran for example, I have shared what information and resources Wings Of The Eagle possesses, to freely provide secure communication and fellowship to believers there.

At one conference I spoke with a Syrian Brother who was telling of the extreme plight of Christians in the environment of ISIS and the armies of world powers. I volunteered the secure communications we could provide and his smile became uncomfortable and he said "we use WhatsApp." WhatsApp? The anti-Christian Facebook owned service? This is what is trusted by the Syrian Church begging for help? I reached out to this Brother afterward and never got a reply. Pretty obvious he didn't trust me. Ok...I shrugged. These things happen.

At a more recent conference, I had a wonderful conversation with the leader of a major ministry working in Iran. You would likely know his name. I asked him what the most pressing need of the Iranian Church is right now, and he said, "Not being connected with one another." I was so excited and he also became excited by the news that my ministry could provide not only secure communication tools but also an online Church environment for them to freely use. We exchanged business cards and he game me the name of an associate of his to call to set up an appointment with him "in the next few weeks," saying he would possibly even fly me out to his ministry headquarters. I wept, thankful to God for this divine connection. As soon as I got home, I followed up with his associate via email and phone and awaited the reply. I waited days and weeks. No reply. I followed up again. And again. Crickets. I reached out to the leader directly. No response.

Not long ago, I reached out to a more secretive ministry in Iran asking what I could do other than send money. No reply. I forwarded our tools and ideas for communication in an extensive message. I finally received the cryptic reply: "we already use something." No "thank you," no other ideas to help with, no "let's talk more later", just dismissiveness. It's not just the rejection of help in all these cases that is hurtful, but the abject rudeness with which it is often delivered. It is flat out un-Christlike. This issue goes beyond any personal sting or hurt over the "dissing" of my ministry, but rather the cold, hard fact that the mistrust among Brothers that is infecting the Body is truly disturbing. The function of this distrust will translate to interior sabotage. This is not the way the Body of Christ is supposed to work. He has not given us a spirit of fear, and we are supposed to be "as one," working together.

WE ARE ALL SUSCEPTIBLE

The temptation to form "cliques" and slink off into our own "vetted" corner of the world is real. The formation of cults around charismatic leaders (Christian ones) has always occurred and will continue. This is something we must not just acknowledge, but we must actively war against it, my friends. God doesn't always send fellow workers who are "one of us." Those of different backgrounds, denominations, and circles travelled in, all will be used by Jesus in the last days. And we had better be welcoming and quick to accept them and ditch the fleshly desire to "be safe." To paraphrase CS Lewis, the Lion of Judah is not a tame lion, but He is good. His Holy Spirit is wild like the wind—such are those born again of the Spirit. And we are all One, ready or not. Hebrews 13:1-2 is quite a challenge to this mindset. "Let brotherly love continue. Don't neglect to show hospitality, for by doing this some have welcomed angels as guests without knowing it."

We aren't even in the proper frame of mind yet to dispense with denominations, though I truly believe that is coming. These examples I have lived though and others I have witnessed are among, basically, the same denomination. What else could this be but immaturity of the Bride? Major intercessory prayer is apparently needed to overcome this stronghold in the Church. It is far too easy, and lazy, to blame "the Catholics" or "the Reformed" or "the Fundamentalists" or "the Church system" instead of actually practicing the unity that our Lord Jesus prayed over us in John 17. If we are unwilling to trust each other, I am fully convinced God will call a whole new set of Saints to do it, even if He has to raise up entirely new believers who know nothing of mistrusting their Family.

For our purposes here, trusting God as the One who calls and qualifies us is absolutely paramount. The Spirit *must* be trusted over and above our fleshly insecurities, tribalism and, yes, greed. Building the physical infrastructure for thousands of Jews in the mountains of Jordan and Arabia will take lots of organization, lots of money, lots of cooperation among the international Body of Christ. This will not be an American effort, nor one merely for the Jordanian or Israeli Churches. Trusting "the stranger" will be unavoidable. Are we prepared to do that? With the Spirit of God ever present in us, there is *every chance of success*.

PART 4: WHAT WE MUST DO

Chapter 10

HEAR WHAT THE SPIRIT IS SAYING TO THE CHURCH

"The Holy Spirit says: today, if you will hear His voice, do not harden your hearts as in the rebellion, in the day of trial in the wilderness"

I hope we have demonstrated that God's Will for His Church's role leading up to and during the time of Jacob's Trouble is plainly laid out in the Bible, and His Spirit is clearly speaking: *we* must do this work and it must begin *now* while it is still day. Some of Israel will flee to the mountains—the Biblical wilderness of Jordan and Arabia—and the Body of Jesus Christ will feed them. We are responsible and accountable to Jesus Himself for doing this final great work.

ENDURING UNTIL THE END: THE VERY LAST DAY

As we detailed in Chapter 7, the Church is to endure in her self-denying, Gospel-spreading mission until the very last day of the age. Before anything else, we need to come to grips with the reality of serving Jesus and His people, Israel, until the very last day. That may be the last day of our mortal lives in the flesh. Or it may be "that Day" when the Father sends the Son from heaven and He splits the sky so the "restoration of all things" can take place. At this juncture it doesn't matter if you believe in a pre-tribulation or a pre-wrath rapture that takes the Church to heaven before the Lord's Return; being prepared to mentally and spiritually endure until the very end is what is required.

One of the most exciting events of this end time drama will be witnessing God's answer to Satan's rage on the earth during the last 3.5 years called The Great Tribulation/Jacob's Trouble. That answer will be the great outpouring of His Holy Spirit as we see Joel 2:28 fulfilled. Plus, the natural consequence of Satan's eviction from heaven will be that the communication line between heaven and earth—for the first time since Adam and Eve—will be *obstruction free.* Can you even imagine the power and impact of direct answers and instructions from the Throne of God? Or of instant angelic assistance? The time described by Daniel and Jesus as "tribulation such as has not been since the beginning of the world, nor ever shall be" will simultaneously be the Church's greatest hour. We will shine the brightest when the darkness is greatest. And the manifest expression of that Light will be in our service to the Jews who heed the warnings we give and flee the land of Israel for the mountains.

WINGS OF THE EAGLE

Here is a short testimony about what can happen if you are highly flawed yet willing to serve. As I mentioned ear-

lier in the book, I launched a ministry online in 2013 and felt the Lord wanted it to be called "Wings Of The Eagle." I knew the name was from Revelation 12, but also I love birds in general and am a fan of the Philadelphia Eagles football team so I figured, what's not to like? The mission of the ministry is three-fold:
1. Connect the Church (worldwide)
2. Save (serve) Israel
3. Preach the Gospel to Muslims

Today at WingsOfTheEagle.com there are Bible studies, webinars, interviews with some well known folks, a blog, a weekly radio/podcast program called Wings Of The Eagle Radio (you can find it on Spotify, Apple Podcasts, I Heart Radio, and Spreaker). We also have started a five minute or less "Prophecy News Update" on YouTube whenever prophetic events warrant. Also an online "academy" of on-demand Bible courses. The flagship is a comprehensive course that is presently over thirty hours in length consisting of twenty-nine different books of the Bible from Numbers though Revelation and eight hot button topics like The Beast/Antichrist/False Prophet, the Great Falling Away, The Rapture and the Millennium. It is called "The End Times For Beginners" but is appropriate for anyone from new Christians through Pastors and Church leaders. I have it on good authority that there is more end-time education in it than is taught in ANY seminary today. The social media engagement has always been of prime importance as well because "that's where the fish are." Wings Of The Eagle now has thousands of subscribers on YouTube and followers on Facebook. Creating viral videos and memes are a big part of that engagement.

As if that wasn't enough, through my burgeoning relationship with Jake McCandless, the Lord led the two of us to try something completely new and a little bit crazy: an online Church. The vision was both for Christians in the West with no church home or who were hungry for more about solid eschatological study *and* for those in other nations who are underground and cannot meet securely or who literally know of no other believers. Thus, Endtime.church was born in the spring of 2018 with seventy people and we are now have a live international worship/teaching/fellowship service every Monday night at 8pm eastern. As a part of that, we have developed a proprietary app in anticipation of social media shutting down Christian discourse. And indeed, this shutting down has already begun. You can get the app free for any iOS, Android, or web browser at endtime.church/app.

Now, the Lord is extending favor among men with invitations to conferences like Understanding The Times and being in documentaries like the forthcoming "Crossroads" with rising Christian star Dana Crosby and contributing to Daniel Secomb's brilliant soon-to-be-released film, "Tears of Jihad." The point is, be willing to be used and watch what Jesus will do!

JACOB'S TROUBLE, MEET JACOB'S REFUGE

While in Israel in 2017, God was up to many things among the people on the tour I was on. From two people who had never met falling in love, marrying and who are now joyfully expecting their first child, to a divine re-connection of pastors from Ashdod and Delaware, to amazing brotherly fellowship with Spirit-filled men from across the Atlantic. Most pressing for me, was the realization that this coming Time of Trouble for Israel was no joke and there seemed to be a dearth of materials and planning commensurate with it. Thus, the seed was planted not only for this book you are now reading but for the next steps. At the inaugural Endtime.Church gathering in March 2019, I laid out the general outline for those steps. Based on the "LET'S DO THIS" response from other members, we started the work. We call it Jacob's Refuge.

The mission of Jacob's Refuge is to provide safe haven for people fleeing after the event known as the Abomination of Desolation. Despite our various end time views, we all acknowledge that Jacob's Trouble will come, and the Jews will need a means of escape. Whenever that time comes, and whoever God has left on the earth to accomplish the task, we have been given due warning in scripture of what will befall those living in Israel, and we have resolved to begin preparation for those who must endure this time. Even if we are not alive, wisdom is the principal thing (Prov. 4:7) and, we believe, wisdom is to begin this process of preparation without delay.

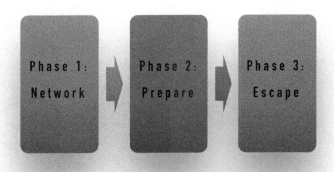

There are three main phases in this effort. Phase 1 is currently underway, and focuses on networking ministries globally and in the region of Israel and supporting their evangelism efforts on the ground. Phase 2, initiated at the start of the Tribulation period as defined by the seven-year covenant, consists of providing "Bug-Out Bags" to Jews in Judea and throughout Israel who are leaving or planning to. This is accomplished through the networked ministries identified and activated in Phase 1. Lastly, Phase 3 will be automatically initiated at the Abomination of Desolation and will involve a predetermined escape route out of major cities in the area to designated safe houses in route to and through the mountains.

Truly, even the most basic common sense in how we prepare for natural disasters and map out escape routes from major storms teaches that it is wise to prepare. God has taught repeatedly in scripture that when disaster comes for His people, He will give them due warning to prepare and to help others. And this, very simply, is the point of all the Biblical warnings about the destruction that will swiftly follow the Abomination of Desolation. When Jesus instructs all those who are in Judea to flee the coming invasion of many armies, we know that, as followers of Jesus, we can make safe havens ready for the massive desperate exodus of refugees.

Because of the political climate of the region, this will require great creativity, secrecy, and a spirit of adventure. We must be prepared to build and to keep this network functioning for generations, as we cannot know the time of the event for which we prepare. Therefore, this ministry will exist largely underground, and must be able to function without constant charitable donation. Through our three-phase approach, we are keeping the primary objective of preaching the Gospel front and center from Phase One until the end, while also providing practical items for a hasty escape in any emergency situation through the "Bug-Out Bag" in Phase Two, and establishing a means of escape in a network of locations along a designated path through the mountains. Jacob's Refuge is a salvific mission, leading lost people to the Messiah, while providing physical means for those fleeing Antichrist's wrath.

We are actively seeking creative individuals, groups and ministries who have a love for Israel and the Jewish people to join us in this refuge mission. Specifically, we are looking for people to cover this project in prayer, know ministries in Israel and the surrounding nations to join our network on the ground, and who can be ambassadors for Jacob's Refuge in local communities. Whatever your abilities, if you have a burden to lend a hand in this project, we want to hear from you. If you have a heart for God's people, a spirit of adventure and the ability to think outside the box, we would absolutely love to hear from you. Please fill out the form at the bottom of the page at JacobsRefuge.com and we will be in touch to discuss details of how you can join this effort.

If you would like to give a financial gift toward this initiative, proceeds will go toward supporting evangelism efforts in Israel, providing Hebrew and Arabic New Covenants throughout Israel and the surrounding nations, and by sponsoring "Bug-Out Bags" to be distributed during Phase Two. Go to wingsoftheeagle.com/donate and select "Tribulation Fund." You can email the team at jacobsrefuge@wingsoftheeagle.com.

LET THE READER UNDERSTAND...THEN STEP OUT IN FAITH

As with any truth in God's Word, proper understanding is just the first step, we must then believe it, accept it, and agree with Jesus. Then, finally, we must apply it, keep it, step out in action. Understanding and accepting that the Church has a responsibility to Israel during the impending final seven years of the age now requires the Isaiah-esque "here I am, send me." No one person or group can do it all, but the supernatural Body of Christ can and will. Are you "in the faith?" If so, let's get to work.

Finally, we come to YOU "the reader". Like I said in the beginning, this book is different. It's not a study or a story with an ending, it may be the opening volley in this particular part of the war. Like all the sermons I preach or messages I share, there is a call to action. Let us all be doers of the Word and not hearers only!

Join in Jacob's Refuge, take the associated Flee To The Mountains coursework, arrange new conferences, invite folks who are tracking in this subject to your church, donate money to the Tribulation Fund, donate your time or property within those mountains to help establish the Where. Let us seek the Kingdom of God and His righteousness together, for the time is near.

SEE YOU AT THE ONLINE COMPANION COURSE

WingsOfTheEagle.com/fleetothemountains

End Notes/Links

The work begins now, sign up to help:
JacobsRefuge.com

Christopher Mantei's ministry site, many free resources:
WingsOfTheEagle.com

Companion course to this book:
WingsOfTheEagle.com/fleetothemountains

Comprehensive on-demand online Bible course:
EndTimesForBeginners.com

Worldwide Fellowship supporting Middle East missions:
Endtime.Church

Jake McCandless' ministry:
StandFirmMinistries.com

Jake McCandless' book "Spiritual Prepper":
SpiritualPrepperStore.com

Joel Richardson's ministry and links to his 6 books including "Mideast Beast" and "Mount Sinai in Arabia":
JoelsTrumpet.com

Mark Davidson's blog and links to his 3 books including "Daniel Revisited":
FourSignposts.com

Fred London's 3 books:
lulu.com/spotlight/fredlondon

Pastor Israel Pochtar's congregation is Beit Hallel in Ashdod, Israel. His ministry page is:
VOJIsrael.org

Ryan Mauro's websites:
DoubtingThomasResearch.com, JabalMaqla.com

Quote from Hezbollah secretary-general Hassan Nasrallah, Oct. 23, 2002:
dailystar.com.lb/News/Lebanon-News/2002/Oct-23/21779-nasrallah-alleges-christian-zionist-plot.ashx

Press release from Saudi Crown Prince Mohammed bin Salman about NEOM:
neom.com/content/pdfs/NEOM-Press-Release-en.pdf

NEOM article from Bloomberg News Jan, 16, 2019:
bloomberg.com/news/articles/2019-01-16/saudi-arabia-to-begin-building-homes-in-futuristic-city-neom

Wings Of The Eagle

JACOB'S REFUGE

EndTime.
Church

Made in United States
Orlando, FL
27 January 2022